Disciples Eldership:
A Quest for Identity and Ministry

By Peter M. Morgan

Eldership Voices, a CD, is an essential part of the course.
Sold separately and available through Chalice Press, www.chalicepress.com,
ISBN 978-08272-08414.

Bible quotations, unless otherwise noted, are from the *New Revised Standard Version Bible*, copyright 1989, Division of Christian Education of the National Council of the Churches of Christ in the United States of Amercia. Used by permission. All rights reserved.

Prayers on pp. 68-69 are from *A Diary of Private Prayer*, by John Baillie, Charles Scribner's Sons, © 1936, Charles Scribner's & Sons. Reprinted by permission of the Gale Group.

Cover Design: Michael Domínguez
Interior Design: Lynne Condellone

Print: ISBN 978-08272-06588
EPDF: ISBN 978-08272-06601
Eldership Voices: ISBN 978-08272-08414 (a CD, sold separately)

www.chalicepress.com

10 9 8 7 6 5 4 3 2 1   11   12   13   14   15   16

Printed in the United States of America

About the Authors

This book was originally a collaboration.

The collaboration began in 1962 when I sat in Dr. Richard Pope's Disciples history class at Lexington Theological Seminary.

Dick Pope knew about elders from more than books: add twenty years, off and on, of eldering at the South Elkhorn Christian Church in Lexington, Kentucky, to his valuable knowledge gained as a scholar.

Neil Topliffe was the second partner in this collaboration. Neil and I had the same group of elders at our first church as ministerial students at Bethany College. Neil succeeded me as pastor of the Chapel Hill Christian Church in Wellsburg, West Virginia. Neil brings the study alive with the CD *Eldership Voices*.

I brought to this original collaboration the influence of some able teachers, the elders who served Marion (Iowa) Christian Church from 1965–1975. They taught me, their pastor, to share ministry with them. Also, I offer to this effort the dialogue with scores of Disciples elders whom I have met in dozens of workshops, seminars, and lectures on eldership across the United States and Canada for the last thirty years.

You have in your hands a revised version of the study originally published in 1983. I am pleased that the work is still in demand and am pleased to update the work by deleting obsolete material and recrafting a few sections based on the experiences of the last twenty years. I do so with greatest appreciation for my original collaborators.

Peter M. Morgan
President, Disciples of Christ Historical Society

Introduction

In the Sunday worship of Disciples congregations, a time comes when an invitation to communion is heard and a communion hymn is sung. During the hymn a group from the congregation comes forward in a kind of processional and takes its place around the communion table. It is lead by two elders who stand behind or beside the table facing the congregation. The moment is still. Then the elders gravely and reverently offer prayers of thanksgiving to God for the gift of Jesus Christ. These are not usually set prayers but are composed by each elder in his or her own way. Even so, certain themes often appear and reappear in them. One often hears, for example, some reference to the bread as emblematic of the body of Christ that was broken, and the wine as representing his blood that was shed for us. When all have been served, the elders and deacons return to their places in the congregation. Thus in a simple, quiet, and reverent service an action is completed that Disciples regard as the very heart of their corporate worship. What is unique in the Disciples communion service is that it requires no ordained priest or minister. For the sake of good order, the Disciples service is normally led by elders who have been elected to this office by the congregation. Elders not only lead in the celebration of the Lord's Supper but have fulfilled other ministerial functions as well, such as serving as teachers, guides, counselors, and as shepherds of the flock and guardians of the faith.

This particular concept of the office of elder did not appear suddenly without preparation or precedent in Christian history. To appreciate and understand fully the eldership today and its long process of development, participants need to study the formative influences. The major concern of this study is to provide a brief interpretation of this history and what it means for the church today in planning for the future.

During the course, *Disciples Eldership: A Quest for Identity and Ministry,* students will seek to establish what the eldership is. The course will then move on to help students know about and perform effective ministry.

Attendance at all sessions of the course is important. The sessions will be two to two and one-half hours in length. Participants will be guided through this resource by the leader, who will be aided by a CD. The designers of the course hope that the commitment and discipline called for by this study will be amply rewarded by the dividends of a renewed ministry.

Peter M. Morgan

A Resource for the Quest

Study Papers
Guidance
Journal Pages

This section of Disciples Eldership is for learners. Study papers and journal pages are to help learners in the quest. Leaders and learners who are studying alone will find guidance starting on page 89.

ITEM TWO

Course Outline

Learner's Section • A Resource for the Quest

Formation

Function

A Message to the Learners

I sat and visited with some people in a congregation. I asked, "Describe your favorite elder." Their portraits:

"She knows and cares about me."

"Joe isn't afraid of taking on tough issues, but he always does it with unquestionable love."

"All Marlis has to do is step up to the Lord's Table and I feel closer to God."

"He came to be with me when no one else was speaking to me."

Elders are mature, although often young, Christian leaders who lovingly lead congregations through crises and conflicts, patiently stand by their people as well as before them at the Lord's Table, and grow in the knowledge of their faith in a thoroughly contagious way.

Two questions in your heart and mind may be the ones I most frequently hear from elders.

1. Why did they choose me?
2. What do elders do?

The first question, "Why me?" shows humility and awe. It is a spiritual question. God does not call us to a ministry and then abandon us. Prayerful reflections on scripture, tradition, and personal experience are the means God uses to address us in our spiritual formation. The first two sections of this study on experience, scripture, and tradition are for our spiritual formation as elders.

The second question, "What do elders do?" will be opened for our discussion in sections three through six. Only after our formation as elders are we ready to address the question of function. Note that there will be no checklist of duties. There will be reflection and conversation to help you work out your faithful ministry with other elders.

This study seeks to foster in elders the best traits possible by helping them discover their ministry as it is now emerging out of its rich tradition.

You and your eldership study group will be using the book *Disciples Eldership*. Each participant will need a copy. The Resource for the Quest section has study papers, plus "reflect and write" pages that may be used and then reviewed as a journal.

A very important companion resource is the CD *Eldership Voices*. I hope you will catch some of the excitement possible in this study in the voices of the elders on the CD.

A Special Message for Individual Students

Although the material is organized for use by a group, it is also usable by you as an individual student.

The simplest procedure is to read the study paper items as you would read a book. The other items which call for reflection and writing may be passed over or used if they have strong appeal. The CD, *Eldership Voices*, could also be a beneficial supplement to your reading.

A more thorough way to do the study is to lead yourself through all the reading and learning exercises. Use the leader's guide in the back of this book and the CD, *Eldership Voices*. It is available from Chalice Press, www.chalicepress.com, ISBN 978-08272-08414.

The most advantageous way of doing the study is to find one or two other individuals who will do the study with you.

Peter M. Morgan

Course Purposes

1. To improve the congregation's knowledge and understanding of the ministry of eldership, and characteristics desired of those in that ministry

2. To foster elders and their congregations in becoming support communities of ministry

3. To help learners to be formed spiritually and claim identity from biblical and historical rootage for the eldership

4. To help learners perceive and practice eldership as a ministry with flexibility

5. To enable learner's to provide knowledgeable and effective ministry as teachers, shepherds, celebrants of the Lord's supper, and overseers

6. To encourage communication and support in ministry among clergy, diaconate, and eldership

7. To offer ways to enrich the life of prayer of individuals and groups

8. To offer guidance for the ongoing life of the eldership

The greatest needs of the eldership are...

SECTION I

Eldership in Scripture

ITEM FOUR

Purposes for Section I

1. To introduce the course and its materials
2. To begin to foster elders and their congregations in becoming support communities of ministry
3. To help learners to be formed spiritually and to claim identity from biblical roots
4. To offer ways to have elders enrich their life of prayer

ITEM FIVE

The Old Testament—A Firm Foundation

To read, underline, and report to your group

Among many primitive peoples and in the earliest forms of religion, the word *elder* usually referred to the older men of the tribe or village. By virtue of their age they were assumed to be wise leaders, counselors, and judges. They were the custodians of the sacred lore and tradition.

In ancient Israel the oldest and most respected served as leaders, counselors, and judges. For example, God directed that seventy Israelite elders assist Moses, who found the burden of leadership too heavy to bear alone as the Israelites wandered in the wilderness.

In the later history of Israel, seventy elders formed in Jerusalem a kind of supreme court known as the Sanhedrin. Each Jewish community and synagogue had its own "little Sanhedrin" made up of elders who had been ordained by the laying on of hands. This latter action symbolized the conferring of the divine Spirit of wisdom and power. In the time of Jesus there was great respect among devout Jews for "the tradition of the elders" (Mark 7:5c).

Thus, in ancient Israel and in other societies as well, the elders were usually the older men of the village, tribe, or society. Indeed, the word *elder* is a literal translation of a Greek word *presbyteros* which means one who is older.

The Greek word is also sometimes transliterated as *presbyter*.

The New Testament—
The Priesthood of All Believers

To read, underline, and report to your group

Prior to the church, Jesus gathered about him a little company of disciples. The total number is unknown, but Paul reported that the risen Christ appeared to more than five hundred people (1 Cor. 15:6). From this "little flock" Jesus had selected twelve apostles, and to them he gave the Lord's Prayer, the Lord's supper, and the rite of baptism as continuing elements in their life together. In a pivotal service on the day of Pentecost this small group was empowered by the Holy Spirit, and the church came fully into being. These earliest Christians became ardently evangelical and were bound to one another in a close-knit community of faith. "They devoted themselves to the apostles' teaching and fellowship, to the breaking of bread and the prayers" (Acts 2:42).

Through the remaining years of the first century the movement spread rapidly through the Roman Empire and to some lands beyond. This remarkable feat of evangelism was not carried out under the direction of a central organization. Although the church in Jerusalem was respected and held in affection, no central office there or anywhere else controlled or directed the rapid growth.

Its advance and spread was largely the work of an enthusiastic and committed membership of unnamed and unknown men and women.

They were not divided into clergy and laity. No priestly class stood between the people and God or was granted exclusive control over the means of salvation. Christ was called "high priest" who became on the cross the sacrifice that once and for all mediated between God and humanity (Heb. 4:14; 7:23–28; and 10:10).

From this perspective Apostolic Christianity was a movement with no distinction between clergy and laity. Insofar as it followed its Jewish parentage, its model was the synagogues and their elders rather than the Temple and its priests. From a sociological point of view, first-century Christianity was more like a dynamic movement than the priestly institution that it would later become. The other side of the coin is that all its members were also described as a "royal priesthood" (1 Peter 2:9), and all shared in the general ministry of the church.

Within this general ministry, the early Christians recognized that there were individuals who had been given certain talents and abilities that fitted them for special ministries. For example, the New Testament tells of apostles, prophets, teachers, miracle workers, healers, helpers, administrators, speakers in tongues, interpreters of tongues, exhorters, contributors, evangelists, pastors, preachers, bishops, elders, deacons, counselors, and others besides (Rom. 12; Cor. 12; and Eph. 4).

These special ministries were sometimes recognized by a service of ordination which involved fasting and prayer and a laying on of hands. To ordain persons was to acknowledge that they had a call from God, had special gifts or abilities, and were accepted by the church (Acts 13:1–3). Further, ordination, it was believed, included a commitment on the part of the ordained and a consecration that conferred a special blessing or grace. Such ordination was not a license to rule but an opportunity to serve.

I T E M   S E V E N

2 John 1—3; 3 John 1—4

Elders Are Teachers

Second and Third John give us glimpses of elders in the Bible teaching the faith. The opening verses alone of these "correspondence courses" reveal John's questing for truth and his joy in the accomplishments of his students. The delight of teaching and learning occurs in those wonder-filled moments of the loving convergence of student, teacher, and subject.

Stephen England and Richard Pope, two Disciples elders/teachers of the mid-twentieth century, instruct us on elders in the Bible who taught:

These men (biblical elders) were the teachers of the congregations. By word, precept, and example of life they led the people to know and to understand what God's revelation of himself in Jesus Christ actually was. By their teaching they safeguarded the churches against insidious heresies, such as that at Colossae, which would have turned Christianity into some strange philosophy of religion. By prayerful experiment, they helped their people to discover what the Christian gospel meant in their moral lives; this was something that no one had ever known, for the gospel was utterly new in the world at that time.[1] —Stephen England

As the church struggled increasingly with problems of order and heresy, it relied more and more on the stability provided by councils of elders, who gave spiritual and moral guidance, presided in worship, and served as guardians of the faith in a society which had in it many competing cults and religions. They functioned as rulers, overseers, teachers, and guardians in the congregations.[2] —Richard Pope

---

[1] Steven England—An unpublished paper.
[2] Richard Pope—A paper written for this resource.

Elders Are Shepherds

Acts 20:17–18, 25–28
Notes:

Scripture to copy and keep where you will read it frequently.

> Now as an elder myself and a witness of the sufferings of Christ, as well as one who shares in the glory to be revealed, I exhort the elders among you to tend the flock of God that is your charge, exercising the oversight, not under compulsion but willingly, as God would have you do it—not for sordid gain but eagerly. Do not lord it over those in your charge, but be examples to the flock. And when the chief shepherd appears, you will win the crown of glory that never fades away. (Peter 5:1–4)

I T E M   N I N E

Elders Are Overseers

Acts 15:1–31
A space for notes on the story as it is told in the class session.

Later Developments—
A Consideration of the Pastoral Epistles

In 1 Timothy and 2 Timothy and Titus, considerable information is given about leadership in the church during the closing years of the first century. Titus was told to "...appoint elders in every town" (Titus 1:5). Elders who ruled well, and were especially effective in preaching and teaching, were to be given "double honor," which apparently meant that they were to receive remuneration for their service. The church thus was moving towards a professional ministry (1 Tim. 5:17). In their discussion of ministry these letters also give a description of the ideal bishop (1 Tim. 3:1–7). The elder should "be above reproach, married only once [in the Greek, "husband of one wife"], temperate, sensible, respectable, hospitable, an apt teacher, not a drunkard, not violent but gentle, not quarrelsome, and not a lover of money" (vv. 2–3). Further, the elder should be well thought of outside the church. Here it should be emphasized that literally and legalistically there are few if any who could qualify for the office of bishop (or elder). For example, women, the unmarried, and those without children would be excluded. Further, such legalism contradicts the basic gospel teaching that Christians of all kinds fall short, and are saved by the mercy of God rather than by any righteousness of their own (Rom. 1:16–17). Indeed, those who think they measure up to this standard may have fallen short; they are at least guilty of conceit.

This statement reflects the particular life situation in which it was written. It lifts up a very high standard of character for leadership in the church which is to be taken not literally, but seriously.

Nancy Heimer, a Disciples minister, adds to our understanding of the Pastoral Epistles:

> While the Pastoral Letters need to be taken seriously by Christians, they also need to be understood responsibly. Written at a time when the coming of the Kingdom was no longer viewed as an immediate reality, these letters were a means of developing a stronger, ongoing religious institution within the society. Christian congregations were increasing in number and spreading geographically. Therefore, it was necessary to strengthen the institution by establishing the line of authority and the responsibilities of the ministers and officers. One question became: "Who is qualified to lead?"
>
> Within the young Christian churches, women, such as Lydia, Priscilla, and Dorcas, had provided significant leadership. Such leadership by church women was without parallel in history and apparently was

disquieting to those men who believed in the patriarchalism of the time. For them it was important to establish that the "place" of women in the congregation was one of silence and submission. In 1 Timothy 2:9–15 there is an indictment against women based on the premise that women did not deserve to be leaders because, through Eve, they had broken God's law. Culminating this statement is the observation that for women salvation is achieved through childbearing! (Is one to make the assumption that no men have ever broken God's law? Do women and men have different bases for salvation?) This argument against the ability of women to have authority is further strengthened in 2 Timothy 3:6–7 where women are depicted as weak, easily subverted by the crafty persuasions of evil men. These "evil men" were believed to lure women into heretical Christian congregations. Yet one wonders if women turned to these heretical congregations, rather than were lured into them, because of alienating attitudes within the "true" congregations.

According to the Pastoral Letters, the one acceptable place where women could continue to serve the church was the "Order of Widows" (1 Tim. 5:5–6). Even that had careful restrictions to determine a "real" widow! Again, to understand the writings of Timothy, one needs to reflect on the situation at that time. "Real" widows, those women who had no sons, fathers, husbands, or brothers to protect and take care of them, were left two sources of economic security: prostitution and the church. The church recognized and accepted this responsibility to women.

Paul's words of assurance that in Christ "there is no longer Jew or Greek, there is no longer slave or free, there is no longer male and female..." (Gal. 3:28) still speak to Christians today. Two-thirds of this message has been heard. Many national, political, and economic differences are no longer barriers to church leadership. Now church people have the opportunity to take the final third seriously and to reopen the doors for primary church leadership to women. Members of the Christian Church (Disciples of Christ), a denomination which so proudly points to the fact that it has ordained both women and men to the ministry for more than a century, cannot continue to deny to women participation as elders and deacons. As women and men are called to serve in the ordained ministry, they are also called to serve in all offices of church life. The challenge to Christians is not to judge but to enable and encourage each individual to use her or his gifts in response to God's call.

Reflections

Take five minutes to reflect quietly on all that you have experienced. You may use some of the suggestions on this page to get started. Notes will help you review your learnings later.

Important new or freshly verified information or insights...

I would like to learn more about...

I'm unclear about...

Reflect on this question:
What have we experienced that will make the most difference for me as an elder or a recipient of ministry from elders?

With All These Witnesses

By faith Abel offered God a more acceptable sacrifice...
By faith Enoch was taken up that he should not see death...
By faith Noah...constructed an ark...
By faith Abraham...went out not knowing where he was to go...
By faith Sarah...received power to conceive...
By faith Moses...left Egypt...
By faith the people crossed the Red Sea...
By faith _____ led me to a fuller life in Christ...
(Hebrews 11 [paraphrase])

Therefore, since we are surrounded by so great a cloud of witnesses, let us also lay aside every weight and the sin that clings so closely, and let us run with perseverance the race that is set before us, looking to Jesus the pioneer and perfecter of our faith, who for the sake of the joy that was set before him endured the cross, disregarding its shame, and has taken his seat at the right hand of the throne of God. (Hebrews 12:1–2)

Unison Prayer

We feel the tremendous responsibility placed before us, Father, as we consider the implications of assuming the role of leaders in your church, we thank you for the lives and examples of those chosen by you as related in your Word. We thank you, too, for the lives of those in our own time, who have led us to a better understanding of the love of Christ through their personal ministries to us.

We are humbled by having been chosen to be shepherds of your flock.

We would ask that you continue to guide and encourage us as we search together for ways of service.

Help us that, through faith, we may attain the strength and courage that comes from loving obedience to the Christ, in whose name we pray. Amen.

—Bill Mitchell

SECTION II

Eldership in the Disciples Tradition

Purposes for Section II

1. To foster elders and their congregations in becoming communities of ministry
2. To help learners to be formed spiritually and claim identity from historical rootage of the eldership
3. To help learners perceive eldership as a ministry with flexibility
4. To encourage communication and support in ministry among clergy, diaconate, and eldership
5. To offer ways to enrich the life of prayer of individuals and groups

I T E M   F O U R T E E N

The Early Church

The story of the eldership continued after the time recorded in scripture. By the end of the Apostolic Age no fixed forms of ministry existed to which every congregation adhered. Nor was there any organization beyond that of the congregation. Likewise, members were not separated into clergy and laity.

Nevertheless, a general movement toward order and discipline took shape. Because of the old, spontaneous, free-wheeling, spirit-filled ministries a more controlled, formalized, and centralized ecclesiastical structure was needed. In some churches that had been led by a council of elders, a bishop began to emerge who functioned to perpetuate continuity of the faith among the elders, deacons, and people. Ignatius wrote of this in 110 C.E. while on his way as a prisoner to die in Rome.

Having a bishop over the congregations was not the plan followed by all churches in the second century. This was indicated by a document called the *Didache* or "Teaching of the Twelve Apostles," written (about 120 C.E.) to serve as a kind of guide to church organization and worship. It directed that bishops (plural) and deacons should be elected to their offices by the people of the congregations. Another document, the First Letter of Clement, written about the end of the first century, seemed to use bishops and elders as interchangeable terms, and to assume a situation in which congregations were ruled by councils of elders. In Justin's First Apology, written about 155 C.E., he described a typical celebration of the eucharist. In his account, the service was led by a "president," probably a bishop who was separate from, and over, the elders and deacons.

Gradually, in the second and third centuries a pattern of organization and worship took shape. In it the bishop emerged as an order of ministry distinct from the elders and deacons. He first ruled a congregation, then a number of congregations in an area or diocese. It is believed that the bishops were the successors to the apostles in unbroken line. Further, in these early centuries, elders (presbyters) were transformed into priests and they and the bishops were given exclusive control over the life-giving sacraments. Meanwhile, the office of deacon tended to become a position on the way to ordination as a priest. Thus in this three-fold ministry of bishop, priest, and deacon there came into the life of the church a separate clerical order, a priesthood, whose members served as mediators between God and humanity.

In this development the bishops became central figures, the focus of power. They controlled (after about 400 C.E.) great wealth. They were advisors to emperors and governors and military leaders. They sometimes lived in palaces. Sometimes they were patrons of the arts. In their cathedrals they sat on thrones like kings.

Although the church became thoroughly clericalized, the idea of a lay elder did not completely disappear. Among the early ascetics who founded the monastic movement were unordained elders who became widely known for their wisdom and insight. Anthony (251?–356 C.E.), for example, left the world to live in the desert as a hermit but in his latter years became widely known as a spiritual director and many people sought him out on his mountain for guidance and help. Some women also became monastic hermits who returned to the world to give spiritual guidance. Theodora (?–491 C.E.) was one of these women.

Soon after the time recorded in scripture the church moved from more spontaneous, free-wheeling ministries toward structures with more _____ and _____. From Ignatius we learn of _____ who functioned to perpetuate the faith among the elders, deacons, and people.

In other situations bishops and deacons were elected and served in each _____.

The pattern that gained dominance in the second and third centuries was of a bishop with oversight of a _____ who was seen as being from an unbroken line of successors back to the apostles. _____ emerged as priests. Thus, in this three-fold ministry of _____, _____, and _____ a separate clerical order came into the life of the church.

The idea of _____, however, did not completely disappear. Some men and women became _____ who went to the desert for solitude, silence, and prayer. They returned or were sought out to give spiritual _____.

The Eldership in the Reformation

Although it was led mainly by ex-priests or monks, the Protestant Reformation was in part a revolt of laity against centuries of domination by the clergy. Martin Luther (1483–1546) appealed to the princes and city magistrates of Germany to reform the church, and it was their support that made the Reformation effective. In three of his best-known tracts, "The Address to the German Nobility," "The Babylonian Captivity of the Church," and "The Freedom of a Christian," Luther argued with rough-hewn eloquence for the priesthood of all believers, asserting that any honorable vocation may be just as religious as that of priest or nun, that laypersons need not be dependent upon the church hierarchy for their understanding of the Scriptures but may read and interpret it for themselves, and that persons are saved by faith through the grace of Christ, and not by the mediating service of the priesthood. Thus Luther prepared the way for laypeople to have a much greater part in the ministry of the church.

All four of the Disciples founders, Barton Stone, Thomas Campbell, Alexander Campbell, and Walter Scott, were originally Presbyterians, and three of them—the Campbells and Scott—had deep roots in the Church of Scotland. It is reasonable to suppose that the Disciples concept of the elder owes much to Scottish religious history. The Scottish Reformation was rooted in the thought of John Calvin (1509–1564) of Geneva.

Holding that the New Testament used the terms elder, bishop, and presbyter as interchangeable words, John Calvin argued for a four-fold special ministry of elders (preaching, teaching, and ruling) and deacons, the last being responsible for the administration of finances and help for the poor and afflicted. In the course of time, this special ministry was compressed into preaching elders, ruling elders, and deacons. They were elected to their offices by the congregation they served.

In Scotland, under the determined leadership of John Knox (1513–1572), Calvinism took root and flourished to such an extent that it became the national church. Knox sought to reform the church "…by a return to scriptural purity in doctrine, worship, and discipline." By scriptural purity he meant that nothing should be brought into the life of the church for which there is no warrant in Scripture. He taught that the observance of the Lord's supper is the central act of Christian worship, and that it should be celebrated each Lord's Day, in a service led by a preaching elder, but with the assistance of lay elders. The latter would also assist the pastor in preparing their people for communion and in seeing that no one partook in an unworthy manner. They would also take communion to shut-ins. They served as teachers. In coordination with the pastor, they would visit among the members, counsel with those in need of help or guidance, and keep a watchful eye on the beliefs and morals of their people. In some cases, it is said, they would patrol the streets at night and enter taverns to see if any of their members were misbehaving, a practice which led to the phrase "elder's hours."

_____ appealed to princes and city magistrates—laypersons—to reform the church. He argued with rough-hewn eloquence for the _____ of all _____, asserting that any honorable vocation is religious and that laypersons need not be dependent upon the church hierarchy for their understanding of _____. They are saved by _____ through the grace of Christ and not by the mediating service of the _____.

_____ was the reformer with the primary influence over the Church of _____, the church of origin for three founders of the Christian Church (Disciples of Christ). Calvin argued for a four-fold ministry of _____ (preaching, teaching, and ruling) and deacons.

The teaching of the Church of Scotland fostered lay elders. They, with the _____, celebrated the Lord's supper each Lord's Day, served as _____, and _____ the members in matters of faith and morals.

Summary of Alexander Campbell's Teaching on Ministry

Alexander Campbell, a founder of the Disciples, helped formulate our church's view on ministry.

Campbell noted three orders of ministry:

EVANGELISTS—
Started Congregations
Evangelized

DEACONS—
Cared for church property
Received, accounted, distributed offerings
Visited the sick

ELDERS—(Bishops)
Taught the congregation
Shepherded the congregation
Guided the congregation

Ronald Osborn summarizes our tradition of the eldership:

The office of ministry in a Christian congregation rested primarily in the eldership, a select body of upright men ordained to preside over the life of the church, to exercise pastoral oversight, to teach the word of God, to maintain discipline, to minister at the table, to set an example to the flock. In a given congregation most, if not all, of these men earned their living at secular vocations. But they were appointed to minister in the church of God.[3]

---

[3] For a full discussion of Campbell's views on eldership see Ronald E. Osborn, "The Eldership Among Disciples of Christ." *Midstream*, Vol. VI, No. 2 (Winter 1967).

The Proud Farmer

by Vachel Lindsay

Vachel Lindsay, a Disciples poet, caught the character of the elder as he described his grandfather in the poem "The Proud Farmer."

His grandfather, E.S. Frazee, was a Disciples elder. He had been a student at Bethany College and later a farmer in Indiana. According to Lindsay "for forty years he saw to it that there was preaching at the Orange Church."

Into the acres of the newborn state
He poured his strength, and plowed his ancient name,
And, when the traders followed him, he stood
Towering above their furtive souls and tame.
. . . .
He lived with liberal hand, and guests from far,
With talk and joke and fellowship to spare,
Watching the wide world's life from sun to sun,
Lining his walls with books from everywhere.

He read by night, he built his world by day,
The farm and house of God to him were one.
For forty years he preached and plowed and wrought—
A statesman in the fields, who bent to none.

His plowmen—neighbors were as lords to him,
His was an ironside, democratic pride.
He served a rigid Christ, but served him well—
And, for a lifetime, saved the countryside.[4]

[4]Nicholas Vachel Lindsay, *General Booth Enters into Heaven and Other Poems*, MacMillan, 1919, pp. 111–113.

Rating Your Congregation's Eldership

What *quantity* of the traditional elder functions is your eldership performing?

Take a moment to reflect quietly and mark each functional area with an assessment number. Use a one (1) to indicate the lowest assessment and a six (6) for the highest assessment.

After giving your number to the tabulator of the group feel free to share your reasons for your assessment with your group.

FUNCTION   My Assessment (1 low to 6 high)

   TEACHING   _____

   SHEPHERDING   _____

   OVERSEEING   _____

Discussion of reasons for our ratings:

Reflections on Section II

Take five minutes to reflect quietly on all that you have experienced. You may use some of the suggestions in this Item to get started. Notes will help you review your learnings later.

Important new or freshly verified information or insights...

I would like to learn more about...

I'm unclear about...

Reflect on this question:
What have we experienced in this session that will make the most difference for me as an elder or a recipient of ministry from elders?

I T E M   T W E N T Y

The Elder in Disciples History

by Dr. Richard Pope

"...where the Spirit of the Lord is, there is freedom." (2 Cor. 3:17b)

The Frontier Context. In the early years of the nineteenth century, Americans of European lineage were moving west in great numbers, settling in the valleys and on the ridges of Appalachia, and pushing on into the rich lands beyond. It was a time of expectancy, of excitement, and of optimism; a time for new beginnings, a time to shake off the interminable quarrels and corruptions of the old world and for creating a new society that could lead the way for all humanity. Or so some of its prophets and seers—Crevecoeus, Emerson, Thoreau, Lincoln, and Whitman—thought.

This new society, which was being carved out of the wilderness at such cost in human labor and hardship, was developing some characteristic attitudes and values. Among these were a love of freedom, a respect for the individual, a pragmatic approach to problems, a suspicion of intellectuals, and a democratic spirit that would say with Scotland's Bobby Burns, "A man's a man for a' that."

On the religious side existed a characteristic reverence for the Bible, a strain of anticlericalism, a tendency toward congregational polity, and a heightened regard for lay leadership in the church. Just as the ancient church developed a monarchial church in a monarchial society, so churches of all kinds have tended to become more democratic in a democratic society.

The Elder in Early Disciples Thought. The Disciples were born into this social context. They had a dream, a vision, of a church united simply on the basis of faithful obedience to whatever is clearly taught by precept or practice in the New Testament. This would lead to the union of all Christians in America and then would follow the unity of the church everywhere, the conversion of the world to Christ, and then the beginning of the millenial age. This would all be done freely and without coercion. Believing that God works through reason, love, and persuasion, they adopted as one of their slogans the statement of Meldenius, one of the Christian humanists of the seventeenth century, "In essentials unity; in non-essentials, liberty; in all things, charity." Obviously, the Disciples owe much to their American environment for both good and ill—and also the Protestant free church tradition as mediated to them by the Independents of Scotland and England, and to the tradition of Christian humanism as mediated by John Locke. This environment and these traditions do not put much emphasis on the distinction between clergy and laity.

The Disciples originated in two separate movements, the "Christians" led by Barton W. Stone, and the "Disciples" led by Alexander Campbell. They united in 1832. Although Stone is in some ways the more attractive person, he lacked the intellectual brilliance of Campbell, and so it is the latter who had the most influence on Disciples thought.

Alexander Campbell believed that Christians are privileged to share actively in the celebration of the Lord's supper and in every other ministry of the church. He further believed that the traditional churches of Christendom were too much under the control of the professional ministry—"the kingdom of the clergy" he called it—and, especially in his early days as a reformer, scathingly attacked "the hireling clergy" for their claims to a special call from God, their love of degrees, honors, and titles, their interest in fees, and their assumption that with their call from God and special education they were set apart from, and above, the laity. Campbell himself early in his ministry had resolved never to take pay for his preaching. A fortunate marriage that made him a man of independent means may have helped him keep this resolution.

As the years went by, and his role shifted from critic to that of responsible leader of a growing movement, he became aware of the need for an educated special ministry to and for the churches. As he read and studied the New Testament he came to believe that it taught that there should be a three-fold special ministry of elders, deacons, and evangelists.

The elders, or bishops as he often called them, should be selected by the congregation and ordained to serve in the special ministry of teaching, ruling, guarding, shepherding, and leading in worship. Deacons, also elected by the people, should serve in managing the material and financial concerns of the church.

Evangelists were also selected and approved by the congregations to go out and preach the Word to those outside the faith, and to help new converts to form congregations. Thus, in theory at least, the elders ministered primarily to those inside the congregation. Evangelists proclaimed the gospel and were generally supported financially by the churches, whereas the elders taught, led, and ruled as non-professionals, that is, they received no remuneration from their congregations.

In actual practice this neat distinction between elders who ministered within the church and evangelists who were commissioned and sent to preach and convert broke down, especially as evangelists increasingly accepted calls to serve as settled pastors of churches. More on this later.

Elders and evangelists were generally ordained to their office by other elders. But this was not an absolute requirement. Disciples have traditionally argued against an "apostolic succession" of ministers through bishops, or a "clerical succession," in favor of an apostolic succession of faith. Thus, ordination, to Disciples, was usually carried out as a matter of good order, but not as something absolutely essential. It did not give some special grace or power to the ordained. Indeed, the early Disciples believed that the very act of recognizing one's gifts to serve as an elder was in itself a kind of ordination. The ceremony of fasting, prayer, and laying on of hands was thus of secondary importance. Here we may also note that ordination was usually for life, and further, insofar as the eldership is concerned it authorized ministry only in the ordaining congregation. In other words, an elder in one congregation who moved his membership to another did not automatically become an elder in his new congregation. Of course, no one could be self-appointed to the office of elder. This could be done only by a congregation.

The Disciples eldership was, then, in the early years of the movement, a special ministry of teaching, ruling, and shepherding by a small circle of men who were elected for life to this office by the congregations they served. They were laymen who served without pay—often with great diligence—and with no theological education but with gifts of faith and natural ability that were recognized by the people in their congregations.

This commission was carried out with such effectiveness that the Disciples movement became in the nineteenth century one of the fastest growing religious movements in the United States, increasing from a handful of people in 1804 to roughly a million by the end of the century. Outstanding among these evangelists were Walter Scott, an immigrant from Scotland who developed "the five finger exercise" to show people in a rational, biblical way what they should do "to be saved"; elder "Raccoon John" Smith, who was short on formal education but long on natural ability; and John T. Johnson, a lawyer who served in Congress and then gave up a promising political career to become an itinerant evangelist.

But while this plan, i.e., lay elders ministering to the congregations while evangelists went out to convert people and form new churches, succeeded in bringing thousands of people to the Christian faith and baptism, it did not provide very well for their nurture and growth in the faith. To put it another way, it taught individuals the "first principles" of the Christian faith (faith, repentance, confession, and baptism), formed them into new congregations, and then left them to the care of elders who were often sincere and well-meaning, but inexperienced and uninformed.

In these early years the lay elders tended to believe that their rule over the congregation included ruling over the evangelists and preachers as well. One such ruling elder wrote as follows concerning their rejection of a ministerial candidate for his church:

Bro. _____: We can't hire Bro. _____ to preach for us.
Some of the members wants him, but we won't have no man what parts his hair in the middle.
Very truly,_____, Ruling Elder.

In their role as guardians of the faith and protectors of the flock, elders sometimes rose to their feet during the course of a sermon and challenged the preacher on some point of doctrine.

The Rise of a Professional Ministry. Evangelists began increasingly to settle down to serve one or more congregations on a regular basis of preaching appointments. But this too was often unsatisfactory. These evangelists/preachers (they not only preached on a basis of regular appointments but also conducted revival meetings) were generally underpaid and had to support themselves and their families by some other vocation, such as farming or teaching school. Further, they usually served their circuit of churches for only a year or two and then moved on to serve other congregations. (One suspects that their "sermon barrel" sometimes contained only thirty or forty well-polished sermons, and that when these were preached it was time to move on.) In spite of their limitations these preachers with their "tent-making" ministry were often wonderfully effective in their service to small, emerging congregations and they deserve to be remembered with gratitude.

As congregations grew some of them became large enough to feel the need for a full-time, resident pastor. As the educational level of their membership increased demand grew for better educated ministers. To meet these needs colleges were founded, beginning with Bacon College in 1836, and Bethany College in 1840.

These schools were liberal arts colleges, with students preparing for the ministry by being given a broad general education in literature, languages, history, mathematics, and science as well as in biblical studies, because it was believed that the future pastors of the church needed this kind of education if they were to serve effectively in their churches and communities. Thus students preparing to be the future interpreters of the Christian faith lived and learned with students preparing for leadership in other areas of service, and they carried out their studies in relation to, and sometimes in tension with, other areas of human knowledge. In keeping with this philosophy of education it has been said that anyone who knows nothing but the Bible doesn't really know the Bible, because the book can be adequately understood only if one knows something of the languages in which it was written and the history and culture out of which it came. Nor can it be interpreted meaningfully unless one knows something of one's own history and culture.

In keeping with this philosophy the first theological faculty designed to educate exclusively for the profession of ministry was the College of the Bible, Lexington, Kentucky (Lexington Theological Seminary today), put in place in 1865, alongside faculties in the liberal arts, agriculture, engineering, teacher training, law, and medicine in the setting of a small university.

A professional ministry was developed against the background of some profound changes that were taking place in American society. Throughout the course of the nineteenth and twentieth centuries greater numbers of people were sharing in the growing wealth of the nation. Their level of education was also steadily moving upward. Through the media of Chautauqua circuits, radio, motion pictures, and television, some measure of culture as well as entertainment was brought to the masses. First high schools, then colleges and universities became accessible to great numbers of youth. Parents with little formal education labored and sacrificed, scrimped and saved, that their children might have a good education. Through immigration from abroad, and through the vast movement of people from farms and small towns to the cities, America became a melting pot, or, perhaps better, a "stew" in which people of diverse ethnic and cultural backgrounds sought to add their particularity to the savory richness of the new pluralism of life in these United States. Through railways, automobiles, and airplanes Americans became a highly mobile people. Because of these and other factors the church had an accelerated need for full-time, professional ministers who could take the lead in meaningfully relating the changeless gospel to a rapidly changing world.

The Disciples were moving from their original frontier and rural background toward the mainstream of middle-class life. The plain little one-room meeting houses that had marked their early years were giving way—like the one-room school houses—to more elaborate structures with carpets, choirs, organs, stained-glass windows, handsome pulpits, beautiful communion tables, candles, formal orders of worship, robes for the minister and choir, Sunday school rooms, fellowship halls, steeples, bell towers, and to the desire to be located on Main Street or the Square or a prominent street in a subdivision.

Such a development naturally called for a settled pastor who could preach polished sermons, lend dignity to a formal order of worship, lead meaningfully in marriage and funeral services, counsel the troubled in a wise and skillful way, and represent the church in the community in a creditable manner.

In effect, the itinerant evangelists moved to the congregations as settled, remunerated, ministers. This phenomenon stirred debate and necessitated adjustment in the old pattern of local church leadership entrusted primarily to elders. In some cases elders welcomed their new professional colleagues as a fellow elder, a first among equals. In other cases the stance was more adversarial.The elders were the rulers who sought to maintain strict control of their newly located preacher.

This growing trend toward a professional ministry in the nineteenth and twentieth centuries did not go unchallenged. Conservatives labored to keep the Disciples locked into the thought and practice of the founders. They believed that the New Testament provided a pattern of ministry that the church was obliged to follow in all generations, and that this true pattern had been discovered by Alexander Campbell and his colleagues in the movement to restore the New Testament church. To these stalwarts determined to walk faithfully in "the old paths," this meant that the "ruling elders" should have oversight not only over the congregation, but over the preachers as well. Many of these conservatives saw the trend toward a professional ministry as a threat to their authority and a digression from scriptural norms. And so they attacked the "one-man system" and spoke contemptuously of "stall-fed preachers," "hireling ministers," and those who accepted the title "Reverend."

Conservatives of this type, even when they accepted the idea of a settled professional pastor for their congregations, felt called not only to work with the minister of the church, but also to continuously review and evaluate the minister's work.

Nevertheless, the trend toward a professional ministry serving as full-time pastors continued to grow steadily with the result that power struggles frequently developed between pastors and elders. In essence the struggle was to see who would have the primary responsibility for leadership in the church.

In this struggle the power gradually shifted away from the elders and toward the minister, and to a more representative body—the church board. The elders might continue to meet occasionally, usually with the minister to discuss spiritual or moral issues facing the church. They served at the Lord's table and they served on the board, but they no longer dominated or ruled the church. The practice also grew of electing elders to a stated period of time—say, three years—after which the elder would go on a "furlough" for at least a year. This rotating method worked against the possibility of concentrating too much power in too few hands. It also enabled more people to participate in the ministry of the church and provided a quiet way of easing a nonfunctioning elder off the board, opening that place of responsibility for someone willing and able to serve. Elders who passed their years of active service often were designated as honorary or emeritus elders.

An effort was made to make the church board as representative as possible of the total congregation and including, wherever possible, old and young, men and women, rich and poor. Membership on the board was often made up of elders, deacons, deaconnesses (later the diaconate), plus the Sunday school superintendent, the president of the Christian Women's Fellowship, and the president of the youth group. Much of the planning and execution of the work was now done by committees such as evangelism, social action, membership development, Christian education, worship, world mission, stewardship, etc.

In this new way of doing things the ordained minister functioned as a kind of executive officer or "enabler" or "minister to ministers" as well as a preacher, teacher, pastor, and counselor. He or she was also expected to provide ideas and leadership in fashioning and carrying out the total ministry of the church, working closely with the committees and the board and sometimes with a pastor's cabinet. In some cases the pastor also worked with the elders, who offered counsel and support on behalf of the pastor and the church. They continued to serve at the table, and also helped the pastor and deacons with visiting and calling.

The above sketch would by no means hold true for all congregations. The role of the elder in Disciples congregations has always been, and continues to be, one of considerable diversity. After all, each congregation is free to follow its own pattern of organization and worship. For example, some elders are ordained for life, while some are simply elected and installed; some who are ordained are thought to belong to the special ministry of the church, while others believe that such persons remain a part of the laity; some expect the elder to do calling and pastoral work with the professional minister while others, in practice, limit their function as elder to offering the prayers at the Lord's table. But in looking back over Disciples history in the last one hundred years or so, a definite trend can be seen: The power of the elders has diminished while that of the board and the professional minister has increased.

But these shifts in power and responsibility are certainly not fixed and final. The church will keep on changing and adapting to new circumstances as do all living things. The functional type of church organization is not forever. No one form of organization is going to be a model for all subsequent generations. James Russell Lowell put it this way in "To Us All, to Every Nation":

> New occasions teach new duties
> Time makes ancient good uncouth;
> They must upward still and onward,
> Who would keep abreast of truth.

Disciples are a practical people, and whatever "works" in making a church more effective in reaching the people of this fast-moving age, and in helping to increase the love of God and neighbor, is likely to commend itself to them, so long as it is not in conflict with the word of God or the Spirit of Christ.

The church continues to change and one sign of this change in the last generation is the electing of women to serve as elders. In Disciples history, as in the history of the church generally, the role of women in the ministry of the church has been a subject that has sparked some controversy. In the early days of the Disciples movement the issue centered on whether women might teach or pray in the public worship of the church. Alexander Campbell took the position that the New Testament forbade women to speak publicly in worship, and this was probably the opinion of most—but not all—Disciples at that time. Nevertheless, women came increasingly to play an important part in the life of the movement. They founded and promoted their own missionary organization with success. In the years that followed the Civil War the first women were ordained and served as ministers, among them Mrs. Sarah McCoy Crank, whose ministry in the Missouri Ozark region demonstrated that women could serve effectively as pastors and preachers. A milestone in this struggle of women was reached in 1952 when Mossie Wyker (Mrs. James) was elected president of the International Convention, an honor that reflected both her own ability as a person and the growing power and leadership of women in religion and in American society.

Better than any polemical argument in favor of women elders is the general feeling that they have brought a new seriousness, grace, and sensitivity to the celebration of the Lord's supper and the pastoral ministry of the church.

What will be the future for Disciples eldership? In the past the office of elder has undergone many changes, and will continue to do so as the church, a living social organism, grows and adapts to a changing world.

Even so, some elements in the history of the eldership seem to continue through all the changes. First, the eldership seeks, and it needs, persons of character and integrity. Inevitably they become examples of Christian living to those who come along after them; thus, the whole "tone" or spirit of a congregation is largely determined by the quality of its leadership.

Second, within the context of the general ministry of all Christians, the office of elder has always carried with it a special responsibility for spiritual guidance and pastoral care. For Disciples, this means that, in cooperation with the professional minister, and under his or her leadership, the elder is concerned for people. Even the elder's prayers at the table are a part of this spiritual concern and pastoral care.

Finally, it must be said that no one person can possibly fulfill all the responsibilities that go with being an elder. The treasures of the Christian faith are contained in earthen vessels, and all are finally dependent upon the grace of God. Nevertheless, those who find themselves in this particular form of ministry are likely to find that the yoke of Christ is easy and his burden is light.

To aspire to eldership is to desire a noble task (1 Tim. 3:1).

SECTION III

As Elders Teach

I T E M   T W E N T Y - O N E

Purposes for Section III

1. To foster elders and their congregations in becoming communities of ministry
2. To help learners perceive and practice eldership as a ministry with flexibility
3. To enable learners to provide knowledgeable and effective ministry as teachers
4. To offer ways to enrich the life of prayer of individuals and groups
5. To offer guidance for the ongoing life of the eldership

I T E M   T W E N T Y - T W O

My Reflections

My most valuable discovery or experience in the last twelve months...

Affirmations of faith I can now make related to that discovery or experience...

Important ideas given to me by my group...

Important ideas given to me by the course leader...

A Community of Teaching/Learning

READING: Find in **Item Twenty-Four** the section "A Community of Teaching and Learning." Read that section as a "pump primer" for starting the flow of your ideas to contribute to the formation of your eldership as a community. Read for up to five minutes.

SILENCE: In silence search for the vision of community God calls your eldership to be.

The silence is an opportunity for God to build up fire within you. If you speak too soon the heat dissipates like the heat escaping through the open door of a steam room. This is a figure of speech from Diadochus, a person who spent much of his life alone in the silence as a "desert father."

He also taught that your contribution through speech will be wiser if it comes through the silence for: "timely silence, then, is precious, for it is nothing less than the mother of our wisest thoughts."

Five minutes is allowed for the silence.

WRITING: Now let your pen flow with your random thoughts on the eldership as community.

When specific action ideas from your reading or from the silence come to you, put them down. You might even want to conclude your writing with a list of specific recommendations.

SHARING/DECIDING:

Teachers in a Community of Growth

Alexander Campbell tells us that a function of the eldership is to teach.

E.S. Frazee was a Disciples elder. He was also Vachel Lindsay's grandfather, described in the poem "The Proud Farmer." Recall from Section II these lines about this godly man involved in the enterprise of learning.

> He lived with liberal hand, and guests from far,
> With talk and joke and fellowship to spare,
> Watching the wide world's life from sun to sun,
> Lining his walls with books from everywhere.
>
> He read by night, he built his world by day,
> The farm and house of God to him were one.
> For forty years he preached and plowed and wrought—
> A statesman in the fields, who bent to none.[5]

The elder as teacher and learner has not always lived with "liberal hand... and joke and fellowship to spare." Some of the more painful moments in our tradition have come from elders who have taken their teaching function as a mandate to be self-appointed definers or orthodoxy and worse: zealous enforcers of their own notions of orthodoxy.

A Community of Teaching and Learning

The eldership today is called to be a teaching community involved in two dimensions of growth:

1. Participants in growth in wisdom and knowledge of the faith by the elders as a separate community and

2. Contributors to the growth in wisdom and knowledge of the faith of the congregation.

Even word choice makes a difference. *Eldership* is preferable to *elders*. Eldership conveys the deeper meaning of community. Elders do not stand apart. They share in a community of ministry called eldership.

Building the community of faith requires time and attention apart from the almost daily cares and tasks of serving as elder. The practice of going apart in a retreat is an excellent opportunity to begin to build understanding and trust and to experience that gift which comes almost unnoticed—a community.

The retreat gives an additional experience that is valuable to the eldership...distance, the opposite of closeness, has value. Distance is valuable in

---

[5] Lindsay, pp. 111–113.

the relationship of ministry to a congregation. Henri Nouwen's words to ministers also apply to elders:

> …sustaining ministry requires the art of creative withdrawal so that in memory God's Spirit can manifest itself and lead to the full truth. Without this withdrawal we are in danger of no longer being the way, but in the way; no longer speaking and acting in his name, but in ours; of no longer pointing to the Lord who sustains, but only to our own distracting personalities. If we speak God's word, we have to make it clear that it is indeed God's word we speak and not our own. If we organize a service, we have to be aware that we cannot organize God but only offer boundaries within which God's presence can be sensed. If we visit, we have to remember that we only come because we are sent. If we accept leadership it can only be honest if it takes the form of service. The more this creative withdrawal becomes a real part of our ministry the more we participate in the leaving of Christ, the good leaving that allows the sustaining Spirit to come.[6]

Distance in proper portion with closeness to those being served has at least three benefits. Distance can help build a close community of the eldership. Distance can help the eldership maintain perspective on the issues and challenges that face the congregation. Distance can allow the Lord of the church to come be present with the people. Elders, after all, aren't little saviors who must solve all problems.

Disciples history has evidence of an uneasy truce between clergy and elders. One promising exception from the past comes shining with possibility in the relationship of elders and clergy today. The clergy and elders can become a community of ministry in the generous spirit that prompted some elders in our past to invite their new young preachers to become first-among-equals with the elders.

Consider the gifts of time, wisdom, knowledge, caring, preparing, preaching, teaching, challenging… all needed to effectively minister to a congregation and, on behalf of the congregation, to minister to the world. It's a rare elder or pastor who can claim enough of all those gifts to minister effectively alone. Ministry is not a solo calling, nor is it management by committee. Ministry is to be shared by those mature lay Christians called elders with those of special training called pastors.

Sometimes pastors will be in giving posture to that surrounding community called "eldership." They may often need to help elders improve skills as shepherds and worship leaders or look together at new information that comes from the pastor's seminary education and/or continuing education.

Just as often, pastors will be in a receiving posture to accept the encouragement, wisdom, insight, new visions, and, yes,…forgiveness of the brothers and sisters of this special called-apart community called "eldership."

The eldership is a community of teachers who come together for mutual enrichment and growth. From their venture as learners they become contagious carriers of an exciting faith.

---

[6] Henri J. Nouwen, *The Living Reminder*. Seabury, 1977, pp. 47–48.

Teachers

READING: Study material in **Item Twenty-Six** under the heading "Contributors to the Growing Wisdom and Knowledge of the Congregation."

SILENCE:

WRITING: Ideas—Recommendations

SHARING: Notes

Contributors to the Growing Wisdom and Knowledge of the Congregation

How is the elder to function as teacher in the congregation? The worst image of our past pictures stern male figures scolding congregations with legalistic "Thou shalts" and "Thou shalt nots." A kinder memory is of the elder with a contagious wisdom luring a people to join in the adventures of discovery, which are enhanced, not threatened, by diversity.

Bob Glover, an elder and leading educator, points in a helpful direction when he talks about the importance of elders as informal teachers as well as leaders in structured settings for learning.

> The church's education, modeled after public education, seems all very good. However, it is not effective unless one knows who one is, identifies oneself with being a part of a particular people, loves being a part of that people, and has a sense of belonging. Then the formal education makes some sense because it is about you, us, and our people and is no longer a foreign subject imposed upon us.

> The story-telling function is crucial. I would like to see the elders assume again more of the teaching style of a tribal elder, sharing with children and young people the stories and heroes of their own people. Elders then function to help persons understand their identity.

> They pass on the stories of the heroes of the tribe. This storytelling helps incorporate persons into their extended family.

How Is the Elder to Teach Today?

The Christian education or nurture department, in most congregations, has primary responsibility for teaching. However, elders can be willing supporters and allies. Some elders may fulfill this ministry by being in the Christian education department or teaching a church school class or being a youth counselor. The experiences of these "in the trenches" teachers will be valuable information to share with other elders.

Not every elder must teach. Some elders' gifts are better given as overseers, or shepherds, but not as teachers. Yet, the eldership has a teaching ministry today when those with gifts of teaching use them in the congregation and help keep other members of the eldership informed about the congregation's teaching ministry.

The example of one eldership may suggest ways in which an eldership can find a fulfilled ministry in teaching. Twelve elders and one pastor make up the eldership of First Christian Church (Disciples of Christ). Seven of those thirteen persons are teachers. The pastor and Jim and Helen planned and led the new members' class for young people this spring. The pastor and Cliff planned and led new member orientations once every four months this year. In addition, Jennifer is a study leader in the Christian Women's Fellowship. Ron teaches the second grade church school class. George has made himself a specialist in church history, including in his repertoire a rich collection of entertaining stories from the congregation. He is called on frequently by classes and fellowship groups for special sessions on the history of the church. The rest of the elders are included in this teaching ministry by the lively stories at elders' meetings from those who are actually teaching.

The eldership is to contribute to wisdom and knowledge of the congregations. Some elders are to use their gifts in the classrooms. Others are to be the informal storytellers who bring alive an ancient faith. All elders are to be knowledgeable about what is being taught in the congregation and to be supportive of the ministry of teaching and learning.

Elders as Learners

READING AND UNDERLINING: Find in Item **Twenty-Eight** the portion you have been assigned, either (1) "Bible Study," or (2) "Worship Leaders and Shepherds" and "Identity with the Larger Church," or (3) "Ideas for Faithful Mission." Take up to five minutes to read the material. Underline recommendations of things to do or important activities to continue for your eldership.

MY SUGGESTIONS: Jot down other ideas to help your eldership grow in enlightenment from Scripture.

SHARING: Put down notes from the ideas and recommendations of others.

Elders as Learners

If elders are to contribute to the knowledge and wisdom of the congregation, they will be students as well as teachers. Learning is an exciting venture in growth of information, insight, application, and skill. The following four topics are areas of learning for the eldership: "Bible Study," "Worship Leaders and Shepherds," "Identity with the Larger Church," and "Ideas for Faithful Mission."

Bible Study

Let the eldership study scripture together. At retreats and other prolonged periods give considerable time to scripture, and also let scriptural study be part of the routine of each gathering of elders. Allow time for the scripture to come alive at each meeting. Scripture is set loose in the midst of the elders in the context of thoughtful and prayerful reflection.

The joy of disciplined scriptural study does not always come easily. A group improves as it stays at the discipline of the study of scripture. Though not easy, Bible study is unsurpassed at keeping present the perception of the church as a people of mission supported by the power and promises of God.

Here is one study design that is aimed to help participants discover maximum vitality in the scripture.

1. Each one silently reads a selected scripture and writes notes paraphrasing the assigned passage. Elders share the paraphrases without implications, interpretations, or generalizations. Definitely no "morals to the story" at this point! Just paraphrases.

2. Participants allow the issues, feelings, and intended meanings of the passage to enter into the gathering of the elders.

   The pastor's skills as a student of scripture can add background, context, and the relation of the passage to the remainder of the book

   Another way of letting the passage enter the elders is through guided meditations in which spoken suggestions lead the imagination to experience the sensations and feelings of the persons in the passage.

   Still another way of "planting the passage in the heart" is to create a quiet time in which each person is responsible for his or her own reflections. For example, an individual may simply select one phrase of the passage for constant silent repetition in rhythm with his or her breathing.

3. Elders pray for enlightenment to perceive from the passage the present will of God. This prayer time may be either shared prayer or private prayer. The purpose of these prayers is to help open the eldership to God's leading. Preaching and moralizing prayers are not helpful!

4. Participants pursue together the query of "from this scripture where do we see how God is leading us and our congregation?"

A couple of hints may help with getting started. These passages are a good way to begin: Matt. 18:10–14; John 10:7–18; Acts 15:1–35; Acts 20:17–38; Rom. 12; 2 Cor. 5; Eph. 2:17–22; 1 Tim. 3:1–13; 1 Tim. 5:17–22; Titus 1:5–9; James 5:13–18; 1 Peter 5:1–4; 2 John; 3 John.

Another idea is to work through a book of the Bible using brief portions at each meeting. A good one for catching a glimpse of God's vision for the church is Ephesians. Another suggestion is to study the Acts of the Apostles.

Worship Leaders and Shepherds

In the ecumenical community the Disciples practice of the Lord's supper is both appreciated and is suspect. The weekly practice of the Lord's supper makes it a centering point for the whole life of the church. This practice continues the worship practice of the first century. That's appreciated. Leaving that most important rite to the administration of persons who may know little of its meaning and its rightful practice is suspect. Disciples would do well to benefit from these suspicions by making the knowledge of the meaning and rightful practice of the Lord's supper a point of concentration as is done in Section V.

A major portion of Section IV is on the shepherding responsibilities of the eldership. The gathering of elders is a good place to practice this ministry. Mistakes necessary to gain competence are made in the safety of the elders' meeting rather than with the persons who can be hurt by our lack of skills. Elders may role-play "made-up" calls with drop-outs or new members. Also, difficult calls that have actually been made may set the stage for role play. It helps to have the elder who was the caller in real life take the part of the one being visited. As trust is built in the community of elders even the tough criticisms become helpful.

Identity with the Larger Church

One desirable trait that an elder is to cultivate is to be "bighearted." Obviously, that means being sensitive and generous and caring of people. Bigheartedness also means a person is rarely trapped in pettiness and is reluctant to think and speak critically of others. Bighearted elders find their identity in the larger church as well as the congregation. The elders are faithful readers of regional publications. They study and discuss business items brought before the Disciples in General Assembly.

Bigheartedness means the elders will be open to give honest consideration to study documents, policies, and practices of denominational units that may be contrary to the opinion of the elders. It also means that the unity of the church is so valuable that the elders lead the congregation to maintain fellowship with the region and general manifestation of the church even when there is painful variance of opinion between the congregation and the denomination. The eldership is to be on the cutting edge of church issues.

Ideas for Faithful Mission

Lyle Schaller has given the church the insight that it is "held together" by unifying forces. These "glues" can be as diverse as a popular preacher, an outside enemy, or a building. One glue is a vivid perception of mission: a clear theological statement, widely known and passionately held in the congregation on why God has called together the people of that congregation and for what purpose they were given life together.

A point of growth for elders may be the leading of the congregation in developing a mission statement. Where a mission statement exists it is the responsibility of the eldership to keep that statement in its consciousness and to lead the congregation in periodic restudy and possible revision of the mission statement.

A central eldership responsibility is to oversee the congregation's faithful implementation of its mission. The section on the eldership as overseer will explore this more thoroughly. A teaching/learning implication of this, however, is that the eldership is constantly to pursue ideas for programs that can stimulate the task groups, functional departments, and fellowship groups in implementing the congregation's mission.

SECTION IV

As Elders Shepherd

Purposes for Section IV

1. To foster elders and their congregations in becoming communities of ministry
2. To help learners perceive and practice eldership as a ministry with flexibility
3. To enable learners to provide knowledgeable and effective ministry as shepherds
4. To offer ways to enrich the life of prayer of individuals and groups
5. To offer guidance for the ongoing life of the eldership

Shepherds

First Peter 5:1–4 is the base upon which to build the ministry of the eldership as shepherds.

> Now as an elder myself and a witness of the sufferings of Christ, as well as one who shares in the glory to be revealed, I exhort the elders among you to tend the flock of God that is in your charge, exercising the oversight, not under compulsion but willingly, as God would have you do it—not for sordid gain but eagerly. Do not lord it over those in your charge, but be examples to the flock. And when the chief shepherd appears, you will win the crown of glory that never fades away.
> (1 Peter 5:1–4)

This passage has Peter, as an apostle, putting himself on an equal level with elders, "as an elder myself." His appeal to the elders is not spoken as a person of authority or higher rank giving orders to lesser authorities on exercising domination over their subordinates. Peter's powerful appeal to the elders is to care for and tend the people of God out of free will and devotion. Attentive caring is a present participation in an emerging way of life full of unfading splendor.

Images

In modern twenty-first century North America, how does the eldership "tend that flock" of God whose shepherds you are? "Shepherds" and "flocks" are word pictures that help inform elders of their ministry. Other images also come to mind.

A friend was reared in a mixed Jewish-Christian home. While reflecting on her childhood she enjoys remembering how her mother fit all the stereotypes of a "good Jewish mother." Mama could tell when Claudia was catching a cold even before Claudia herself knew she was catching a cold.

"Claudia, you're not feeling well."

"Mama, I feel fine."

"Claudia, eat your chicken soup. Tomorrow we're going to be ahead when you catch a cold!"

Elders have many of the traits of a "good Jewish mother." Jewish mothers know when their children are going to get sick even before it happens. The elders come to know their portion of the congregational family so well that problems are recognized even before they occur. Both show a close attentiveness to those special people called family.

The "gatekeeper" is a second image of the elder personally caring for a portion of the congregation. All gates are watched. The elders watch over the whole congregation but no one elder has to watch all the congregation. The coming and going of people is noted. Church membership is not static; rather, each person is in motion—either being more attracted to the church or moving away from involvement in the church.

Medieval gatekeepers gave newcomers directions. "This is where you buy chickens." "Mass begins at 11:00." Introductions were made. People left the city, some in anger, some out of necessity. The gatekeeper noticed and was the last person with a chance to defuse the anger or to send the sojourner on with a blessing. Today's elders offer a ministry of being loving gatekeepers.

"Shepherds," "Jewish mothers," and "gatekeepers" each add to our understanding of the caring function of the eldership. All point to an eldership with an essential trait: people who "mind" or pay attention in a caring way to a group of people for whom they accept responsibility.

SECTION IV   I T E M   T H I R T Y - O N E

Category	Description	Needs	Persons Who Come to Mind	The Ministry of the Eldership
A	**Active** • Attend Worship • Appreciate the church • Support with finances • Accept responsibilities • Overcome discouragement • Are not defeated by conflict	• To be thanked • To be heard • To have expectations and desires seriously considered • To be known and cared for as persons of value • To be informed of hopes, dreams, issues, goals, and plans of the congregation		• To say "thank you" • To know and care for these persons by listening to both hurts and hopes • To report "feedback" to the eldership • To help shape future programs because of some of the "feedback" • To acknowledge special times of celebration, such as birthdays and anniversaries • To be present at times of stress, such as death in family, illness
B	**Becoming Less Active** • Less frequent worship attendance • Critical comments • Letters of resignation • Slipping away unnoticed	• To be responded to promptly • To be listened to without judging		• Pay attention to worship attendance patterns • Respond promptly to attendance changes • Go to listen, not to defend • Ask to be forgiven when appropriate

C	**Dropouts** • No longer active • No worship attendance in at least one year • Time, money, interest reinvested in family and/or community • The pain of dropping out has been sealed over rather than resolved • Persons often screen out attempts to reopen wounds received at the time of dropping out	• Patient, caring, listening	• Build trust through listening • Don't defend • Ask to be forgiven when appropriate • After trust is built, renegotiate relationship with the congregation
D	**Becoming More Active** • New members • Persons with recent life-changing event • Increased worship attendance • More financial and volunteer support	• Supportive person for help in assessment, goal setting, strategizing • Supportive attention on progress toward goals	• Early visit for story listening, encouragement, and goal setting • Quarterly follow-ups for one year
E	**Never Active** • Never attends, never gives • Never moved from membership to fellowship with congregation • Often transferred inactivity from previous congregation	• To catch the vision of life enriched by being a person of faith • To experience vital faith as it is expressed in a congregation	• Listen to person's faith journey • Do the work of an evangelist
F	**Shut-In** • Does not attend worship or other activities of the church • Confined to home because of ill health or because of need to care for one another • Is interested in and supports the church by such means as are available: reading, prayer, phone visits, money	• Worship experience with persons of the congregation • Ways to overcome isolation and loneliness • News of the community • Ways to feel useful to others	• Become the church present by sharing in worship • Bring news of the church • Run errands • Encourage persons when possible to be in ministry through prayer, reading, and phoning

Preparing for a Call on New Members: A Training Sample for Elders

New member calls are often most enjoyable. These people are positive about the church and eager to discover ways of relating to the congregation. Spending time with new members is important. An evening with a family may help them set their own goals for involvement in the congregation.

In your preparation learn the stages in a new member call.

A. Introductions

B. Get-Acquainted Conversation

C. Listening to Their Story

D. Role Clarification

After expressing welcome and appreciation for their membership, say that as "their" elder you want to help them make their church membership a long and valued relationship. What is done in the first year is often crucial to the success or failure of valued church membership.

In this visit indicate to the family that you wish to work together in setting goals for the family's involvement in the church.

E. Goal-Setting and Empowerment

In ministry to new members you are a "spiritual director" helping them be in charge of their own lives within a congregation. Your tone is to be supportive rather than commanding. Three goal areas are to be the focus of the evening:

1. Ask, "What goals do you want to set for yourself in sharing religious experiences and nurture with the congregation?" You can lead the family to specific statements of such things as frequency of worship attendance and participation in a prayer group.

2. Suggest that the family set for itself ways to find close personal friends in the congregation. Here you can give them names of persons with common interests. Also, you can encourage such specific goals as attending church night suppers, inviting other church families to attend sporting events, etc., with them. These activities will not guarantee friendships. However, they are settings in which the gifts of friendship may occur.

3. Ask, "What groups in the congregation are in a ministry you find important enough to share?" Here you may need to describe the possibilities. Help the individuals to set their own goals for participation in a limited number of these groups. Ministry is directed toward two areas. The first is ministry within the church—choirs, church school youth groups. The second is ministry from the church to the world—evangelism, social action. Help the new members make their choice of involvement on the basis of knowledge of both kinds of groups.

F. Arranging Future Visits and Leave-Taking

State that you would like to visit again in a few months and ask if it is all right to call ahead to arrange that visit.

Again, in the follow-up sessions, be careful not to judge less-than-perfect progress. Come simply as a friendly supporter helping the new members be clear on their self-accepted intentions about church membership.

Write one or two sentences that you might use to make transitions between each stage in the call.

Introductions

Get-Acquainted Conversation

Listening to Their Story

Role Clarification

Goal-Setting and Empowerment

Arranging Future Visits and Leave-Taking

Graph of One New Member Call

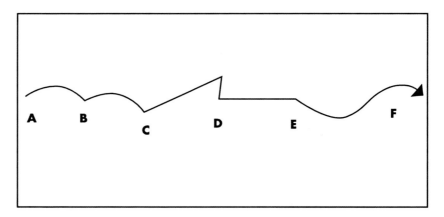

Line indicates feeling of caller about the call. (For example, line moving up indicates positive feeling, high energy; line moving down means call is becoming bogged down, caller is frustrated, feeling negative.) Letters indicate the stages of the call as listed on pages 54–55.

I T E M   T H I R T Y - T H R E E

Observer

You are to observe a practice call of an elder on new members in your church. To prepare for your assignment familiarize yourself with the material being studied by the elder, **Item Thirty-Two**, and read through this Item. You will not speak during the call. In fact, you may need to be five or six feet from the action so that you will be more of an outsider. After the call you are to share your observations.

Draw a graph modeled after the one in **Item Thirty-Two**. Note what was happening at the transition points.

_____ = feelings   letters = transitions

Report Words and Behaviors

The Elder	The New Members

After the call, take about two minutes to share your comments and allow three minutes for discussion.

You may want to do a little coaching with your ideas when the elder shares his or her feelings about rough spots in the call.

I T E M   T H I R T Y - F O U R

Shepherds

READING: Study material in **Item Thirty-Five**, "A Way to Shepherd the Congregation and a Plan for Training."

SILENCE:

WRITING: Ideas—Recommendations

SHARING: Notes

A Way to Shepherd the Congregation and a Plan for Training

Organization helps the church to be more thorough and consistent in bringing the love of Jesus Christ to persons.

An organized shepherding plan helps the church live out the love of Christ in such a way that those are touched who are most frequently overlooked.

The purpose of being a community of love is primary. The organization that helps carry that love is secondary and is to be as simple as possible.

Responsibilities of the Shepherds
   Flock size—Twelve families

1. Occasionally review material in **Item Thirty-One.**

2. Call on each family at least once a year with no objective except to build a relationship with them and to listen (no pledge calls or recruitment calls here, please).

3. Phone or send notes to families on special occasions: birthdays, graduations, weddings, making the honor roll.

4. Be present at times of distress: ill health, loss of job, death in the family, etc. Do what you can to help in such ways as arranging for food to be brought in to the family.

5. Visit families promptly when there is a change in worship attendance pattern. This helps prevent dropouts.

6. Lead worship in the homes of the shut-ins of the flock at least once every three months. Include the Lord's supper.

7. Visit new members quarterly.

8. Be active in prayers of intercession for each person in your flock every week.

Some people enjoy being together in a flock to socialize or to engage in study or projects. Be willing to help if your flock wishes to come together. This approach, however, is strictly optional. Your shepherding is not to be determined by the amount of interest in having a flock group.

Other tasks that need to be done:

The Task	Suggestions for Who Does It
1. Take individual worship attendance and mail monthly reports to elders	Persons selected by the membership department
2. Classify all the families by A, B, C, D, E, or F (see **Item Thirty-One**) according to their participation	A subcommittee of the membership department whose members know the people of the congregation
3. Shepherd the shepherds	The pastor or a designated elder
4. Train the shepherds	The pastor or a designated elder
5. Lead the shepherds in being a support group	The pastor or a designated elder
6. Create a climate of acceptance of shepherding as a way to increase the congregation's ability to be a community of love	The pastor and/or a designated elder through announcements, newsletters, articles, and letters, and introductions and prayers at worship services

The Training

You may use portions of monthly meetings to learn about characteristics and needs of members and to practice skills in responding to those needs. Each meeting may focus on one of the categories in **Item Thirty-One**.

Additional training past the six categories may be held for hospital visits, calling when death occurs, and shepherding absentee members such as military persons, college students, etc.

SECTION V

*As Elders Celebrate
the Lord's Supper*

Purposes for Section V

1. To foster elders and their congregations in becoming communities of ministry
2. To help leaners perceive and practice eldership as a ministry with flexibility
3. To enable learners to provide knowledgeable and effective ministry as celebrants of the Lord's supper
4. To offer ways to enrich the life of prayer of individuals and groups
5. To offer guidance for the ongoing life of the eldership

I T E M   T H I R T Y - S E V E N

Folk Priests

Power, clarity of purpose, firm resolve, the unburdening in forgiveness—consider the effects of the Lord's supper on devoted worshipers. God achieves these benefits through a pattern of symbols: words of institution, prayers, bread, wine or grape juice, eating, drinking, and those serving the meal. Yes, the elders are a powerful part of the system of symbols for the worshipers. Listen to a worshiper overheard commenting on an elder, "The witness of her life is so valuable to me! When she comes to lead me to communion I see clearly the source of her kindness and I am drawn by her to that source."

Disciples elders as "folk priests" represent a full expression of the cherished notion of the priesthood of all believers. They are called from the congregation as mature Christian leaders. They are not paid for church services. They do not live in their community because they were given a call to serve the church in that location. Few have specialized formal education in ministry or are set apart by rites of ordination. Rather, from a gathered congregation, men and women of godly character are called and set apart by that congregation to perform the priestly functions for that congregation. Hence, Disciples elders are in fact "folk priests."

"Priest" is appropriate terminology. The long-term presence of specific elders in a congregation helps establish the church within a rich tradition of dependable ministry through the passing generations. In some communions that same value is claimed in apostolic succession or the historic episcopate. One Disciples elder, with maturity of thirty years as an adult church leader with seven ministers, said, "My service in the eldership brings continuity to ministry. I've stayed after each pastor has left."

The elder as priest escorts the worshiping community into communion with God. Bringing people and God together involves movement from God's side and from the people's side. From God's side comes the fulfilled promise of being present. The elder simply orders the rites of the meal to allow the presence of God to come into vivid awareness for those who share at the table. The movement of the people toward communion is aided by the elders serving as priests as they lead the congregation in prayers of thanksgiving and as they silently bring the people before God in intercessions during the meal. The elder/priests have outward actions during the Lord's supper such as speaking, leading prayers, and dispersing the bread and wine to the deacons for serving the congregation. The elder/priests also have the inward action during the meal of holding in consciousness the needs of the people before a merciful and empowering God.

ITEM THIRTY-EIGHT

Worship

O God, you are my God, I seek you,
    my soul thirsts for you;
My flesh faints for you,
    as in a dry and weary land where there is no water.
So I have looked upon you in the sanctuary,
    beholding your power and glory. (Ps. 63:1–2)

The psalmist helps the people express what is deep in their hearts. As a desert thirsts for water, so they long for God. It is in the sanctuary that they often encounter God!

What happens when people congregate to be encountered by the mystery and grace of God?

They participate in an ancient practice. Christian worship has rootage in the services of the synagogues and the Temple of ancient Israel. The worship of the early followers of Jesus was recorded in Acts 2:41–42: "So those who welcomed his message were baptized, and that day about three thousand persons were added. They devoted themselves to the apostles' teaching and fellowship, to the breaking of bread and the prayers." Disciples frequently note the conformity of their orders of service with this worship of the early church.

Again, continuity with ancient practice is evident in a description of worship in the second century written by Justin Martyr:

And on the day called Sunday, all who live in cities or in the country gather together to one place, and the memoirs of the apostles or the writings of the prophets are read, as longs as time permits; then, when the reader has ceased, the president verbally instructs, and exhorts to the imitation of these good things. Then we all rise together and pray, and, as we before said, when our prayer is ended, bread and wine and water are brought, and the president in like manner offers prayers and thanksgiving, according to his ability, and the people assent, saying Amen; and there is a distribution to each, and a participation of that over which thanks have been given, and to those who are absent a portion is sent by the deacons. And they who are well to do, and willing, give what each thinks fit...[7]

What happens when people congregate to be encountered by the mystery and grace of God?

They share a four-part event: gathering, receiving the Word, responding in faith and thanksgiving at the Lord's Table, and departing to serve God's world.

The gathering recognizes the individuality of each person. Each one is distinctive but comes to enrich the whole community's affirmation and praise of God. Some people need to make contact with other people. They will often be in animated conversation outside the sanctuary. Other people need a quiet atmosphere in which to center their attention on God. Others appreciate having the worship leader explain the theme of the service or even rehearse hymns and responses prior to the call to worship.

The service of the Word sets loose within the church the message of God. A significant amount of scripture reading is heard. The Word may be presented musically. The scripture is painted in the varied hues of personality in preaching. Lectionaries are now used with more frequency as the basis of the service. The lectionary prescribes the specific weekly readings at public worship. This three-year cycle helps the church hear a significant portion of scripture and also helps make the public readings representative of the whole Scripture.

The service of the Word is also coordinated with the anniversaries of the Christian year. The people, enlivened by scripture, are renewed as they annually re-experience the preparation for Christ's birth, the birth itself, Epiphany, etc. As wedding anniversaries may be renewing to marriages, so the anniversaries of God's mighty acts are to be renewing to the church.

In the Lord's supper the people participate with God, who generates faith and thanksgiving in response to the Word. An offering is presented: bread, wine, money, commitment, labor...God transforms that offering. The bread and wine embody the memory of Jesus Christ, the presence of Jesus Christ, the hope of sharing a future great banquet with the risen Lord. Money, commitment, and labor are transformed into gifts that contribute to God's kingdom now and in the future.

Those of the congregation who gather to hear the Word and celebrate the Lord's supper are empowered to intercede for each other and the world and are then released to go minister.

What happens when people congregate to be encountered by the mystery and grace of God?

---

[7] *Ante-Nicene Fathers*. The Christian Literature Publishing Co., 1887, p. 186.

The psalmist nudges into words the answer of the heart:

Because your steadfast love is better than life,
    my lips will praise you.
…you have been my help,
    and in the shadow of your wings I sing for joy.
    (Ps. 63:3, 7)

NOTES:

ITEM THIRTY-NINE

The Lord's Supper

The most consistent function of elders throughout Disciples history has been as presiders at the Lord's Table. In some congregations that is the totality of the elders' ministry. It is a rare exception when the elders do not administer the Lord's supper. Two things are overseen by elders at the table. First is the linking of the congregation to its source of life, God made known in Jesus Christ. Second is the proper conduct of the rites of this service of worship.

Professor Keith Watkins' book, *The Feast of Joy*, brings help for elders in understanding the communion service.

The major act of Christian worship is a meal, a feast of joy where Jesus is the host and His people everywhere the guests. When the church first began, this table fellowship was the focus of their life together…In our own time this ceremonial meal continues to be the most important form of worship offered up to God by those who trust in Jesus.[8]

The meal, now stylized and formalized, takes the emotions generated by biological life and transfers them to the interactions of groups of people. When we eat, we feel happy, relaxed, confident; and when eating becomes a ritual these same feelings become attached to our group associations. Happiness becomes joy, relaxation becomes peace, confidence becomes trust. All is based on the salvation which God achieves in Jesus Christ and is experienced and in company with others similarly blessed. Thus

---

[8] Keith Watkins, *The Feast of Joy*. The Bethany Press, 1977, p. 11.

the natural delights of eating are transferred to our group associations which become infused with these qualities.

This relatively simple transfer of emotion is complicated by the nature of the ingredients of the meal. In the Lord's Supper we eat bread and drink wine, but from the church's earliest years these simple foods are perceived through the lenses of Jesus' own words. While holding bread, he said "my body given for you," and while holding the cup he said "my blood shed for you."

The transfer of emotional power is thus intensified. Blood is the sign of life itself and any meal that calls attention to blood evokes a very strong emotion of personal involvement. Thus the Lord's Supper is an especially intense example of the mealtime transfer of personal feelings to the activity and meanings of groups. What does the shedding of blood signify? Pain and sacrifice, courage and honor, love and devotion. These qualities of life are transmitted to the community that gathers in the name of Christ when they eat and drink bread and wine, flesh and blood.

This dual foundation for meal imagery has contributed to a long-term ambivalence in the emotional character of the Lord's Supper. Sometimes the delight of natural feasts has been stronger, sometimes the dreadful fascination that is associated with all of life's blood experiences. Even in New Testament times this contrast was present. Joyful exuberance may have been the earliest quality. Christians met together "with glad and generous hearts" (Acts 2:46), excited because Jesus had risen from the dead. He joined them in their meals, making their joy even greater. With this beginning, the unrestrained festivity described in I Corinthians 11 is understandable. The party was getting out of hand. What the early church was forgetting, Paul brought back to mind with his sober emphasis upon Christ's suffering. His theology of the cross tempered the church's excessive merriment at communion.

Yet from that time the two strains continued: the Lord's Supper as joyful feast of the saved, the foretaste of the Lamb's bridal feast in heaven (Revelation 19:6–10) and the Lord's Supper as remembrance of his passion and participation in his death.[9]

Dr. Watkins later recites two hymns as he discusses the Lord's supper being an event of companionship between God and people. In these hymns note the two strains of the feast, the more somber remembrance of Christ's passion and death, and the more joyful foretaste of the Lamb's bridal feast in heaven (Rev. 19:6–10).

---

[9]Ibid., pp.18–19.

Let All Mortal Flesh Keep Silence

Let all mortal flesh keep silence,
And with fear and trembling stand;
Ponder nothing earthly minded,
For with blessing in his hand,
Christ our God to earth descendeth,
Our full homage to demand.

Deck Thyself, My Soul, with Gladness

Deck thyself, my soul, with gladness,
Leave the gloomy haunts of sadness,
Come into the daylight's splendor,
There with joy the praises render
Unto him whose grace unbounded
Hath this wondrous banquet founded;
High o'er all the heavens he reigneth,
Yet to dwell with thee he deigneth.[10]

The Words of Institution. This recital of the scriptural words states under whose authority this meal is shared. The words of institution are normally spoken by either the pastor or an elder who has been set apart by the congregation for this purpose. Passages that may be used include Matt. 26:26–28, Mark 14:22–24, Luke 22:17–20, or 1 Cor. 11:23–25. The words of institution may be included as part of the communion prayer, at the time of the breaking of the bread, or as part of the approach.

The Approach. These shared meditations of the elder or pastor, or these words of scripture, invite the worshipers to the table. The words give recognition that the people are approaching the table with an offering and God is already present at the table with a greater offering.

The Offering. The offerings from the people, usually money, are brought forward and presented to God with a prayer of thanksgiving.

The Communion Prayer. Dr. Watkins describes the function and nature of this prayer:

"The communion prayer brings all of the service into focus. It praises God for his glory and mercy, for his gift of life in Jesus Christ, and for his life-giving Spirit. In this prayer leaders of the congregation ask God's help for all Christians who want to respond to him in loving service." [11]

The Breaking of Bread and Distribution. The loaf is lifted to be in plain view of the people and is "fractured," often accompanied by the words, "His body broken for you." The chalice with wine or grape juice is lifted and presented with arms extended, often with the words, "His blood spilled for you." The bread and wine are then distributed for the consumption, nourishment, and communion between the worshipers and God.

[10] Watkins, p. 27.
[11] Watkins, p. 115.

The Conclusion. Brief final words of scripture or phrases of thanks–giving conclude the meal. This is often effective when said or sung by the congregation. [12]

I T E M   F O R T Y

Prayer Vigil

"Spiritual leaders of the church" often describes the elders as they oversee the congregation by functioning as folk priests. This richness of the priestly ministry is far more than being a ceremonial custodian of the central rite of the church. The elder's own spirituality is a gift to be brought to the act of presiding at the table.

Both the elder's life and the leadership at the Lord's supper are to be intensely and intentionally godly—not self-righteous, but godly. The elder who is growing in consciousness of God in all of life because of rich spiritual experience in private prayer and meditation will illumine consciousness of God in others.

A growing spirituality may depend upon a set time of daily prayer. Priests of other traditions say daily offices. The Disciples tradition has no book of offices. Disciples elders may need to begin cultivating similar habits of spirituality by using the resources at hand. Here is one possible pattern:

Set aside a quiet place and time.

First, relax and let God take away the cares and tensions you bear.

Second, read scriptures or prayers of some great devotional literature. John Baillie's *A Diary of Private Prayer* is a good resource for beginning daily prayer.

Third, with eyes closed, center your mind on some phrase or object of devotion. You may, for example, become clearly aware of an image of Jesus with the children of the earth. It is a time of adoration.

Fourth, bring into the presence of the caring God people of special need. Include in these intercessions your pastor, church leaders, and members for whom you are shepherd.

Fifth, conclude your "offices" with a prayer of thanksgiving.

Many persons find that keeping a journal is a great help in developing a life of spirituality.

The life of a "spiritual leader" does not come easily to most persons. There will be dry periods. Keep coming back. Let yourself be ready when God is ready to

---

[12] The author is indebted to Keith Watkins for his work *The Feast of Joy* for this discussion of the parts of the Lord's supper. The author recommends that elders use this book for additional discussion on the actions in the Lord's supper as well as a resource for suggested prayers.

come near. Your life of compassion is more full because of prayer. Your private and public prayers as "folk priest" at the table become richer because you have been enriched by God in your personal times of prayer and meditation. You do not come empty to the congregation in the spiritual work of the table. That spiritual work is led out of the abundant overflow of your personal prayer life in the fertile times. In the dry times of personal prayer the urgency of your longing will be evident at the table. As priest, your prayers and your life of compassion are to be contagious to the people with whom you humbly share the bread of life.

Go now to your prayer vigil. You may use the steps listed above in your time of solitude, silence, and prayer.

After relaxing and breathing away your tension, you may wish to take into your inner space one of the prayers printed below. You may wish to write some thoughts or prayers as you close your vigil.

Prayer for a Sunday Vigil

> Holy Spirit of God, Thou who are a gracious and willing guest in every heart that is humble enough to receive Thee, be present now within my heart and guide my prayer.
>
> For all the gracious opportunities and privileges of this day, I give Thee thanks, O Lord:
>
> For the rest I have this day enjoyed from the daily round of deeds:
>
> For thine invitation to keep the day holy to Thyself:
>
> For the house of prayer and the ministry of public worship:
>
> For the blessed sacrament in which, as often as we eat and drink it, we remember our Lord's death and taste His living presence.
>
> For all the earthly symbols by which heavenly realities have today laid firmer hold upon my soul:
>
> For the books I have read and the music which has uplifted me:
>
> For this day's friendly intercourse:
>
> For the Sabbath peace of Christian homes:
>
> For the interior peace that has ruled within my heart.
>
> Grant, O heavenly Father, that the spiritual refreshment I have this day enjoyed may not be left behind and forgotten as tomorrow I return to the cycle of common tasks. Here is a fountain of inward strength. Here is a purifying wind that must blow through all my business and all my pleasures. Here is light to enlighten my road. Therefore, O God, do Thou enable me so to discipline my will that in hours of stress I may honestly seek after those things for which I have prayed in hours of peace.
>
> Ere, I lie down to sleep, I commit all my dear ones to Thine unsleeping care; through Jesus Christ our Lord. Amen.[13]

[13] John Baillie, *A Diary of Private Prayer*. Charles Scribner's & Sons, 1936, p. 135.

Prayer for a Vigil on Other Days

O Thou Creator of all things that are, I lift up my heart in gratitude to Thee for this day's happiness:

For the mere joy of living:

For the sights and sounds around me:

For the sweet peace of the country and the pleasant bustle of the town:

For all things bright and beautiful and gay:

For friendship and good company:

For work to perform and the skill and strength to perform it:

For a time to play when the day's work was done, and for health and a glad heart to enjoy it.

Yet let me never think, O eternal Father, that I am here to stay. Let me remember that I am a stranger and pilgrim on the earth. For here we have no continuing city, but we seek one to come. Preserve my by Thy grace, good Lord, from so losing myself in the joys of earth that I may have no longing left for the purer joys of heaven. Let not the happiness of this day become a snare to my too worldly heart. And if, instead of happiness, I have today suffered any disappointment or defeat, if there has been any sorrow where I had hoped for joy, or sickness where I had looked for health, give me grace to accept it from Thy hand as a loving reminder that this is not my home.

I thank Thee, O Lord, that Thou hast so set eternity within my heart that no earthly thing can ever satisfy me wholly. I thank Thee that every present joy is so mixed with sadness and unrest as to lead my mind upwards to the contemplation of a more perfect blessedness. And above all I thank Thee for the sure hope and promise of an endless life which Thou has given me in the glorious gospel of Jesus Christ my Lord. Amen.[14]

My Journal:

---

[14] Ibid., p. 91.

Presiding and Praying at the Lord's Table

One of the most frequently expressed desires of elders who lead at the Lord's Table is to function effectively. A common comment along with "I am not worthy of this task," is "What am I supposed to say and do at the table?"

Items Forty-One and **Forty-Two** are intended to help with the question, "What am I supposed to say and do?"

Style of presiding will be discussed. Suggestions for common placement of the words of institution will be offered. The communion prayer will receive extra attention.

Style of Presiding. Alexander Campbell gave a word that almost universally characterizes the style of those who celebrate the Lord's supper in the Christian Church (Disciples of Christ). His word was *simplicity*. "The manner of celebrating the supper...graceful, easy, artless, and simple."[15]

The elder is communicating God's action by gesture. Those gestures are not to be rigid or regimented or rushed or pompous or excessively grand. The reaching, walking, breaking bread, offering the elements, handling of trays, speech, and contact with other worshipers is to be "graceful, easy, artless, and simple."

Of course, the gestures of the elder are to reflect what is in the heart of the elder. The heart can be free of anxiety if the elder is familiar with the mechanics of the service. The elder is to be invested in consciousness of Christ present as he is remembered while bread is broken, wine poured, and prayers offered. The elder is also to be aware of his or her own feelings of thanksgiving as Christ's presence is experienced with the congregation. The elder may find even mechanical gestures of serving have authentic meaning when silent prayer is being offered for the congregation while celebrating the Lord's supper.

Words of Institution. Professor Keith Watkins' book *The Feast of Joy* is an excellent resource for individual elders or elderships as they prepare to celebrate the Lord's supper. This study item will use Dr. Watkins' book.

Three of the Gospels and 1 Corinthians recount the establishing of the Lord's Supper. Jesus is described as taking up the bread, giving thanks to God, breaking it, and giving it to the Disciples. In similar manner he handles the cup. Even in their biblical form these passages give the impression that they had long been used in the regular worship of Christians. There is other non-biblical evidence that from ancient times these words of institution were part of the service. In our own time this language continues to be used, either in one of the New Testament forms or in a combination of two or more of them.

---

[15] Alexander Campbell, *The Millennial Harbinger Extra No. II*. 1830, p. 86.

There are three places in the communion service where the words of institution are likely to occur: as part of the approach to the table, in the text of the communion prayer, and as part of breaking of bread prior to the distribution to the congregation.[16]

The eldership in dialogue with the pastor is to determine where the words of institution will be offered. The following are four possibilities from the Bible to use as the words of institution.

While they were eating,
Jesus took a loaf of bread, and after blessing it
he broke it, gave it to the disciples,
and said,
"Take, eat; this is my body."
Then he took a cup,
and after giving thanks
he gave it to them, saying,
"Drink from it, all of you;
for this is my blood of the covenant,
which is poured out for many for the
forgiveness of sins." (Matt. 26:26–28)

While they were eating,
he took a loaf of bread, and after blessing it
he broke it, gave it to them,
and said,
"Take; this is my body."
Then he took a cup,
and after giving thanks
he gave it to them, and all of them drank from it.
He said to them,
"This is my blood of the covenant,
which is poured out for many." (Mark 14:22–24)

Then he took a cup,
and after giving thanks he said,
"Take this and divide it among yourselves;
for I tell you that from now on I will not drink
of the fruit of the vine until the kingdom
of God comes."
Then he took a loaf of bread, and when he had given thanks,
he broke it and gave it to them, saying,
"This is my body, which is given for you. Do this in remembrance of me."
(Luke 22:17–20)

…the Lord Jesus on the night when he was betrayed
took a loaf of bread, and when he had given thanks,

---

[16] Watkins, *The Feast of Joy*, pp. 94–95.

he broke it and said,
"This is my body that is for you.
Do this in remembrance of me."
In the same way he took the cup also,
after supper, saying,
"This cup is the new covenant in my blood.
Do this, as often as you drink it,
in remembrance of me." (1 Cor. 11:23b–25)

The Communion Prayer. Professor Keith Watkins offers these comments on the communion prayer:

The communion prayer brings all of the service into focus. It praises God for his glory and mercy, for his gift of life in Jesus Christ, and for his life-giving Spirit. In this prayer leaders of the congregation ask God's help for all Christians who want to respond to him in loving service.

In the free tradition to whom this manual is addressed the prayer is short, prepared new for each occasion, and free to express the widely varying sentiments of the congregation. This tradition presupposes that the congregation is already united with the living Christ and that the prayer is the conversation that results. Ordinarily the prayer mentions the bread and wine and suggest a relationship between these elements and Christ's body and blood given for us. Yet this tradition forces no obligations upon the prayer, either of form or of theological content.

The prayers (are to us a) pattern…thanksgiving, remembrance, calling upon the Holy Spirit, rededication of life to his service. In many congregations the custom is that two such prayers are offered, one for the loaf and one for the cup. In other congregations only one communion prayer is offered.[17]

---

[17] Ibid., pp.115–116.

Preparing Communion Prayers

The elder preparing to pray at the table is to express the thanksgiving of the church for the life, death, and resurrection of Jesus Christ. The parts of the prayer are thanksgiving, remembrance, calling upon the Holy Spirit, and the rededication of life.

Notice how each of the themes is present in the following prayer:

Thanksgiving

Creator of all that is, we praise you:
> For your own self, beautiful and filled with light;
> For your works, incredibly varied and fruitful;
> For life itself and consciousness with which to enjoy it.

Redeemer of all creation groaning in travail, we praise you:
> For your justice that holds us to the standard that all things created are good;
> For your mercy that forgives and renews us when we fall short;
> For your promise that all things will be made new.

Remembrance

Most of all we praise you for Jesus Christ:
> Through him you created the world;
> By his life and ministry you showed us your nature;
> Because of his suffering and death you saved us;
> By his resurrection you gave us power to live.

We bring you these gifts of bread and wine to be a sign of our gratitude, O God, for all that you are and have done for us in Jesus Christ.

Calling upon the Holy Spirit

As we eat the bread and drink from the cup of salvation, renew in us the presence of your Holy Spirit.
> Cleanse us from sin.
> Restore us to new life.

Rededication

And then send us into the world as signs of your creativity and agents of the redemption that you are bringing.

Through Christ we pray. Amen.[18]

In this second prayer, write the appropriate theme on the line in the margin:

Lord, for the signs of your powerful and surprising presence we give you thanks:
> The steady coming and going of the seasons;
> The constant productivity of the earth;
> The dependable cycle of life;
> The irrepressibility of love and forgiveness in the face of evil.

Even more we thank you for Jesus Christ who fully expressed your majesty and immediacy.
> At this table, set with our gifts of gratitude, we remember him:

[18]Ibid., p. 116.

His gentle and quiet life;
His charismatic presence;
His singular sense of divine vocation;
His faithfulness against all odds.
And we praise you that by his sacrifice he showed us your nature
    clearly and powerfully.
By your Holy Spirit:
Open our eyes that we may see you face to face;
Enliven our bodies that we may touch and handle things unseen;
Unlock our wills that we may accomplish the work you give us to do.
In the name of Jesus Christ. Amen.[19]

Write a communion prayer using the themes in the margin. You may wish to base the prayer on a lesson from the lectionary such as Matt. 10:26–33 (Fifth Sunday after Pentecost—Cycle A).

Thanksgiving

Remembrance

*Calling upon the
Holy Spirit*

Rededication

---

[19]Ibid., p. 117.

Recommendations and Personal Commitments

What are the most important learnings from this section?

What benefits are possible for our congregation from this section?

What recommendations do I have from this section for our eldership?

What personal commitments do I wish to make because of this section?

SECTION VI

As Elders Oversee

Purposes for Section VI

1. To foster elders and their congregations in becoming support communities of ministry
2. To help learners perceive and practice eldership as a ministry with flexibility
3. To enable learners to provide knowledgeable and effective ministry as overseers
4. To offer ways to improve the life of prayer of individuals and groups
5. To offer guidance for the ongoing life of the eldership

Overseeing

The Disciples eldership has had three functions: (1) teaching, (2) shepherding, and (3) overseeing. If overseeing is understood to mean ruling or governing the congregation, then clearly it is the most changed of the three functions since the early days of the Christian Church in the first half of the nineteenth century.

An Australian Disciple responded to a request to characterize American Disciples elders. He said, "They seem to me to be ceremonial figureheads." Immediately the queen of the United Kingdom and Commonwealth came to mind.

If Disciples elders are figureheads, then our predecessors who fought to diminish the elder's autocratic power to dictate policy and set practice in congregational programs have been excessively successful. It is true that rotating boards and functional departments have increased congregational participation in decision making, and that's good. It is true some elders were dictatorial. As recently as the 1935 International Convention (now General Assembly) of Disciples, ministers were expressing concern over "the domineering elder who arrogates to himself popish powers as he insists on ruling the flock of God." That speech would now, it most places, be irrelevant, and that's good.

The emerging Disciples eldership is now finding appropriate ways to oversee by sharing spiritual insight, by articulating its vision of the congregation's mission, by giving evaluation and support to congregational programs in a pastoral style, and by linking the people of the congregation to the source of their vision and strength in leadership at the Lord's Table.

Sharers of Vision

To share a vision one must have a vision. The capacity to dream and to see potential new directions is increased when elders alternate being involved and being detached from the everyday issues of parish life. The congregation needs the support of and help of the elders in the practical decisions of raising money, recruiting volunteers, repairing the building, etc., etc., etc. However, elders who become saturated in those issues and tasks without times of detachment are jeopardizing their capacity to perceive the visions of possibility in mission. They, thereby, deprive the congregation of the valuable gift of the vision of new possibilities. The eldership ministers well as overseer when it clearly articulates and shares within its own group and with the congregation the fruits of its prayerful seeking and its inspired imagination.

Vision often begins in prayer. The elder will do well to let melt away the tensions of a class to teach, a call to make, a report to give, a worship service to prepare, a Bible study to lead…in short, all of the demands of ministry. In letting the motor of activity come to idle, the elder may then word his or her own form of this prayer: "God, you have given us so much—in what ways are we as a congregation to respond in gratitude? O Lord, inspire our ministry!"

Inspired Imagination. Hope fuels acts of ministry. Hope comes alive in being lured and enticed by exciting possibilities. Let those with good imaginations pour out hopes and dreams. "In my inspired imagination I perceive that God wants our congregation to enrich our community by giving to others the great treasure we have in our life of faith. I see a loving people clearly articulating the stories of their faith." "I see our congregation making a great impact on some people who think no one cares as we develop a prison ministry." "In my mind's eye I perceive our people becoming informed about and adding to the worldwide effort to protect human rights for all." When God inspires our imagination, listen, take notes—even in the middle of the night. You are to prepare to share with your brothers and sisters in the eldership the vision you have for your congregation.

Shared with Other Elders. The hopes and dreams of the elders are to be tempered and shaped by sharing with fellow elders. The eldership is made up of women and men who come together to tell of their visions and dreams for the church. That sharing is to be a testing of the dreams. Some dreams are not worthy of enactment. Other dreams are stored until their time comes. But in the sharing there are some dreams that become contagious to the group of elders. These visions of possible mission energize or animate the eldership. The dreams become gifts of the eldership as they carry out their ministry of being overseers. Elders then become carriers to the congregation of contagious visions.

Clear Articulation. What are some ways to share the eldership's vision of ministry with the congregation? Some public times of sharing include sermons during worship, prayer periods at board meetings, guest columns in the congregation's newsletter. Private opportunities are also available. One excellent setting is to meet with each committee chairperson prior to annual planning sessions. The elders' dreams can be "pump primers" that activate the chairperson in pushing back the limits on what is possible. Hold your dreams loosely. Let the congregation shape, refine, and even reject them.

Helpful Evaluators. To oversee is to come together with persons with programmatic responsibility to evaluate, to make course corrections, to give guidance, to express support and appreciation. In a typical meeting one or two of the elders will sit down with a chairperson of a functional department—Christian education for example. The first task is to let the chairperson know that the elders are friends and not adversaries. Begin by having the chairperson assess progress and also share impediments, frustrations, and disappointments. Inquire as to what goals or strategies need to be rethought. Offer advice, encouragement, or specific help for the problems. Truly celebrate the victories that have been won. These sessions are usually helpful two or three times a year.

The elder as overseer does not hold a title without responsibility. The overseer elder today is a loving, supportive critic to those who carry the responsibility of the programmatic ministry of the congregation.

One way to organize for this task of evaluation is to have one or two elders assigned to each functional department. The elders could arrange periodic meetings with the chairpersons to give support. At each gathering of the eldership there would be scheduled brief reports on how each department was "living out the vision." Some more difficult and crucial issues may take longer discussion by the elders and may have the chairperson of the department visit the elders' meeting. Again it is crucial not to give orders or directives but to be a friendly resource for the chairperson to use in dealing with his or her own issues.

I T E M   F O R T Y - S I X

READING: Study material in **Item Forty-Five:** "Overseeing"

SILENCE:

WRITING: Ideas–Recommendations

SHARING: Notes

Deciding Our Ministry: Elders Teach

As the church struggled increasingly with the problems of order and heresy, it relied more and more on the stability provided by councils of elders, who gave spiritual and moral guidance, presided in worship, and served as guardians of the faith in a society which had in it many competing cults and religions. These elders functioned as rulers, overseers, teachers, and guardians in the congregations.[20] —Richard Pope

Recommendations	My Score	Our Score

---

[20] From Dr. Pope's study paper for Section I of this course.

Deciding Our Ministry: Elders Shepherd

Now as an elder myself and a witness of the sufferings of Christ, as well as one who shares in the glory to be revealed, I exhort the elders among you to tend the flock of God that is in your charge, exercising the oversight, not under compulsion but willingly, as God would have you do it—not for sordid gain but eagerly. Do not lord it over those in your charge, but be examples to the flock. And when the chief shepherd appears, you will win the crown of glory that never fades away. (1 Peter 5:1–4)

Recommendations	My Score	Our Score

Deciding Our Ministry:
Elders Celebrate the Lord's Supper

The richest service of all was when [the old church at Bethany] had a sermon by Mr. Campbell followed by Dr. Richardson [a lay elder] at the Lord's Table.

Never did high priest enter the holy of holies with more genuine reverence than did Dr. Richardson enter upon his duty on these occasions.[21] —Dwight Stevenson, Cloyd Goodnight

Recommendations	My Score	Our Score

---

[21] Cloyd Goodnight, Dwight Stevenson, *Home to Bethpage: A Biography of Robert Richardson.* Christian Board of Publication, 1949, p. 164.

Deciding Our Ministry: Elders Oversee

The office of ministry in a Christian congregation rested primarily in the eldership...[a select body of men and women who] preside over the life of the church..., exercise pastoral oversight..., teach the word of God..., maintain discipline..., minister at the table..., set an example to the flock.[22] —Ronald Osborn

Recommendations	My Score	Our Score

---

[22]Ronald E. Osborn, "The Eldership Among Disciples of Christ," pp. 82–84.

Prioritizing: What Areas of Ministry Are to Receive First Attention?

You have one hundred points to spend in backing specific recommendations you wrote in **Items Forty-Seven** through **Fifty**. Your points will help the eldership decide their future ministries.

Use the column "My score" on **Items Forty-Seven** to **Fifty**. Remember the rules:

Give points by specific recommendations, not pages or categories.

No page is to get more than 35 points.

The total of the four pages is not to exceed 100 points

The column "Our Score" is used later for recording the total group's decision.

Reflecting on Disciples Eldership

A Quest for Identity and Ministry

Take four minutes to reflect quietly on all you have experienced. You may use some of the suggestions on this page to get started. The notes you put down may be used later as you wish to check your growth as a person in ministry.

Important new or freshly verified insights...

I would like to learn more about...

I'm unclear about...

Reflect on this question:
What have we experienced in this course that will make the most difference for me as an elder or as a recipient of ministry from elders?

Closing Comments

Read silently these summary comments.

The elders of the Christian Church (Disciples of Christ) are part of a strong tradition of ministry. In fact, they have historical precedence over Disciples clergy. As such they have been witnesses to the one who was called the Good Shepherd and Rabbi as they have given oversight to, shepherded, and taught people in the congregations.

One pessimistic assessment of the eldership is that it is now a mere shadow of its former self. The power struggles against the clergy and changed congregational structure have left the eldership with the consolation prize of being merely ceremonial functionaries in worship services.

However, stronger images of the elder as someone other than "a mere shadow" do come to mind. Like a sailboat that shifts its sails to run swiftly and beautifully before the changing wind, so also has the style of elders shifted over the years. Few elders are left who define orthodoxy in their own terms and cruelly impose it on others. Thank God. Many elders now contribute to the nurture of the congregation. Thank God again. Few elders are left who dictate congregational policy and practice. Many lead the church in such a way that the people perceive their mission and make their way toward it. Therefore, let us not lament any losses of the eldership but rather marvel at the flexibility with which it "shifts its sails to run swiftly and beautifully before the wind."

Elders have found new styles of serving as overseers and teachers. They have found the quality of their ministry enhanced as they have welcomed women into eldership. It is an eldership that shines with promise as it discovers the joys of spirituality—a spirituality that equips people to be "folk priests" and shepherds of the flock of God.

Through our history God has given the gift of flexibility to the Disciples order of ministry called eldership. With that flexibility the eldership, begun by its pioneer ancestors, stands on the edge of the future. The promise is that congregations of the Christian Church (Disciples of Christ) will be ably taught, lovingly shepherded, and spiritually supported.

Unison Prayer

Eternal Father God, we pray that you [will] help us to be more thoughtful and sensitive to the needs of others. We realize as your children we will have days of difficulties. In these days may we seek your guidance that whatever is done, is done according to your will. In the name of him who taught us to pray…Our Father who art in heaven…
—David Brown

A Guide for the Quest

Course Design
Session Outlines
Suggestions for Leaders

This section of Disciples Eldership is for leaders. Specific suggestions for learning activities are given for each section. The learner's section is found at the front of the book.

Course Outline

Leader's Section • A Guide for the Quest

Formation • A Quest for Identity

Function • A Quest for Ministry

A Message to the Leaders

In preparation for each session you, as a leader, will be using this printed study guide as an orderly sequence of steps during the sessions. The material is organized into six sections. Some groups may complete a section per session. Others will use more than one session to finish some sections.

The CD, *Eldership Voices*,* is an integral part of these study materials. I hope you will catch some of the excitement possible with this study through the voices of the elders and others on the CD. They will provide you with insights and questions as you prepare and lead the group. The voices on the CD are called voice impressions, and are for use during the sessions with your eldership group. The voice impressions for each session are in sequential order and listed on the printed sheet accompanying the CD. The introduction to the CD gives you more details on the use of the CD for your preparation and for use with the group.

You and your eldership study group will also be using the learner's section of this book. Each participant will need a copy. The resource has study papers, plus "reflect and write" sections that may be used and then reviewed as a journal.

Options are available to you on when and where to offer this course. For example, you may go through the course in six to nine monthly sessions of two and one-half hours each. Weekly sessions are possible, and have the advantage of getting the participants out into fuller action much sooner. Retreats offer the advantage of developing deep caring relationships. All options in this course assume that elders will continue to support each other's growth in ministry in monthly meetings. Later, an outline will be suggested for use in these meetings. An annual offering of the course soon after congregational elections will incorporate and train new leaders.

A wide choice of study groups is possible:
  congregational committees
  eldership groups
  district or regional study groups
  clergy groups
  college or seminary classes
  one or two interested individuals

Eldership Voices, ISBN 978-08272-08414, may be ordered from Chalice Press, www.chalicepress.com (1-800-366-3383).

The study has a total of six sections:
—Eldership in Scripture
—Eldership in the Disciples Tradition
—As Elders Teach
—As Elders Shepherd
—As Elders Celebrate the Lord's Supper
—As Elders Oversee

The emphasis of the study you are leading is on eldership today, yet yesterday is still with us. Eldership is a living, changing, emerging ministry, but rooted within its past. This study attempts to connect the excitement of present new styles of ministry with the spiritual formation of prayerfully knowing the past. From the past we will use Alexander Campbell's three functions of the biblical elders (teachers, shepherds, overseers) to describe the contemporary eldership. If Mr. Campbell were to study along with your group he might see some things he could never have imagined in the early decades of the nineteenth century. During the course he might also recognize some of his influence bequeathed to us: a people seeking to live out a biblical ministry with integrity.

You have an important assignment in enabling a vision of the ministry of eldership. I pray that your hard work will be rewarded by seeing your elders become a community who, because they grow in relationship with God and with each other, are capable teachers, priests, shepherds, and guides of your congregation.

Peter M. Morgan
President, Disciples of Christ Historical Society

Course Purposes

1. To improve the congregation's knowledge and understanding of the ministry of eldership, and characteristics desired of those in that ministry

2. To foster elders and their congregations in becoming support communities of ministry

3. To help learners to be formed spiritually and to claim identity from biblical and historical rootage for the eldership

4. To help learners perceive and practice eldership as a ministry with flexibility

5. To enable learners to provide knowledgeable and effective ministry as teachers, shepherds, celebrants of the Lord's supper, and overseers

6. To encourage communication and support in ministry among clergy, diaconate, and eldership

7. To offer ways to enrich the life of prayer of individuals and groups

8. To offer guidance for the ongoing life of the eldership

A QUEST FOR IDENTITY

Eldership in Scripture

Purposes for Section I

1. To introduce the course and its materials
2. To begin to foster elders and their congregations in becoming support communities of ministry
3. To help learners to be formed spiritually and claim identity from biblical roots
4. To offer ways to have elders enrich their life of prayer

Materials

1. CD player
2. *Eldership Voices* CD with **Voice Impression 1** cued
3. A copy of *Disciples Eldership* for each participant
4. Pencils
5. Chalkboard and chalk or flipchart, markers, and masking tape
6. Bibles—at least one copy for every two people

Steps in Section I

Step 1 • 10 minutes   Purpose #2
Coming Together
Cluster participants into groups of four. (If there are six or fewer keep them together in one group.) Spiritual formation comes, in part, from prayerful reflection on our experiences. Have each person share with his or her group either (1) a significant moment when an elder brought the ministry of Christ to him or her, or (2) his or her most fulfilling experience of ministry as an elder.

Step 2 • 10 minutes   Purpose #1
Introduce the Course
Begin this section by playing **Voice Impression 1**, "What Is an Elder?" using the CD *Eldership Voices*. Follow the taped comments by asking the group to think of the first images that come to mind when you say the word "elder." Build upon this beginning by giving one or two minutes of simple and clear description about the course and welcome the participants. In preparation you will need to read "A Message to the Leaders" (pp. 90–91), plus listen to the introduction and **Voice Impressions 1–4** on the CD, *Eldership Voices*. Jot down a couple of ideas from that material for use in your welcoming remarks. Remember, keep it brief!

Give out the "tools" of the course. Explain that the group will be helped in its work by the book, *Disciples Eldership*. Have them read the introduction, which is **Item One**.

Another tool will be the voice impressions on the CD. **Voice Impression 1** used above was one example of these audio resources. Others will be mini-lectures, elder comments, and meditative quotes. These voice impressions will be used throughout the study sessions to provide information and stimulate discussion.

Have the participants find the course outline and course purposes, **Items Two** and **Three**, in the *Disciples Eldership*. Read aloud the outline and purposes. This would be an excellent time for the learner to read "A Message to the Learners," pp.6–7.

Step 3 • 15 minutes   Purposes #1, #2
Groups React
Have each person reflect quietly on the course purposes, **Item Three**, and check the purposes about which they have the most interest or excitement. Assign by name the person closest to you in each group to report the tabulation of checks for each purpose. After about one minute have each person share with the group his or her choices. Tell groups after four minutes of sharing that they only have one minute left.

Next, have each individual take one minute to complete at the bottom of **Item Three**, "The greatest needs of the eldership are..." After these reflections, assign the same reporter used above the responsibility of recording and later reporting the upcoming conversation to the total group. Let the groups know that they have five minutes for all to share.

Have the total group hear the report of tabulations and individual needs. Newsprint will help you keep a record that you may wish to display during the entire course.

Step 4 • 1 minute   Purpose #4

Prayer

Offer the following prayer:

> This is the day that the Lord has made, let us rejoice and be glad in it. Father, we thank you for this day and for all of the many blessings you have so richly bestowed upon us.
>
> As we meet to study and prepare ourselves to learn about the eldership of the church, we seek your presence and guidance. Speak to each heart, mold us and fill us with your Holy Spirit, and lead us in new ways of bringing the good news to a needy world. Joy to the world, the Lord has come. Amen.
>
> *Mary Fugate*

Your study group may be interested in knowing that all prayers in this resource are written by elders.

Step 5 • 2 minutes   Purpose #3

Introduce Purposes of Section I

Have participants find **Item Four** in their resource. Read through the section purposes.

Step 6 • 15 minutes   Purpose #3

Reading/Reporting on Study Papers

Have each person in the group number off "1–2, 1–2," etc. Number "ones" are to read and underline key phrases in **Item Five**. Let them know that they will be reporting to their groups on what they read in "The Old Testament—A Firm Foundation." At the same time the "ones" are reading **Item Five**, the "twos" are to be reading and underlining **Item Six**. They are to share information they have discovered in "The New Testament—The Priesthood of All Believers." In sharing they will talk about such questions as, "What were key ideas that stood out from your reading?"

After nine minutes stop the reading and have the "ones" report to the "twos" of their small group. When they have finished, or after three minutes, have the "twos" share with the "ones" what they have read.

Step 7 • 5 minutes   Purpose #3

Bible Study on Elders as Teachers
   Begin Step 7 by stating that one function of elders in the New Testament was teaching. Write "Teachers" on the chalkboard or chart.

Functions of the Eldership
1. Teachers

   Distribute Bibles and have participants read the opening verses in 2 and 3 John. Read in unison the opening paragraph of **Item Seven**. Two Disciples scholars are quoted in **Item Seven** of *Disciples Eldership*. Ask for two volunteers who will read the quotes aloud.

Step 8 • 10 minutes   Purpose #3

Bible Study on Elders as Shepherds
   Select a person you know to be a good public reader and have him or her read Acts 20:17–18, 25–28 while others follow along.
   Encourage the participants to tell you what is happening in the scene and what is being said.
   Introduce **Voice Impression 2**, "Acts 20: Setting the Stage," and suggest that participants use **Item Eight** to take notes on the Acts 20 passage.
   End Step 8 by writing "Shepherds" on the chalkboard or chart.

Functions of the Eldership
1. Teachers
2. Shepherds

   Then suggest that of all the biblical material suitable for elders to memorize, many select 1 Peter 5:1–4 as the best. Have the groups find the text in **Item Eight** and read it in unison.

Step 9 • 15 minutes   Purpose #3

Bible Study as Elders Are Overseers
   Have each participant read Acts 15:1–31. Make sure that you are thoroughly acquainted with the text. After five minutes have the total group give you all the important facts of the passage. Let them know before they begin that drawing conclusions, morals, or generalizations from the text is out of bounds.
   At this point you only want facts. Suggest that participants prepare to jot down facts in **Item Nine** as they are reported. As they listen you may need to use a prodding question such as…
   In what city does the story begin?
   Where does it end?
   A controversy is evident—who are the parties in conflict?

What is the issue that divides them?

What process is used to resolve the conflict?

Who are the key persons in settling the issue?

What is the final decision in settling the dispute?

What counsel is given at the conclusion of the story?

Finish this step by having the group listen to **Voice Impression 3**, "The Elders Help Guide the Church."

Write on the chalkboard or newsprint...

Functions of the Eldership
1. Teachers
2. Shepherds
3. Overseers

Step 10 • 10 minutes   Purpose #3

Later Developments in the New Testament

One difficulty in understanding the eldership relates to the Pastoral Epistles (1 & 2 Tim. and Titus) in the New Testament. These books are often quoted by those wanting to exclude women from the eldership. Your group may be helped by reading **Item Ten** in *Disciples Eldership*. The silent reading should take about four minutes. After all have finished reading introduce Nancy Heimer by saying that, *"While the Pastoral Epistles reflect the customs of the early centuries of the church, it is beneficial to our study to hear the viewpoint of a woman today who reflects on the same passage."* Play **Voice Impression 4**, "Another Voice on Pastoral Epistles."

Step 11 • 15 minutes   Purpose #3

Quiet Time

Give your group some time to absorb, integrate, challenge, appreciate (whatever they wish to do) all the material they have covered in Section I. Have them turn to **Item Eleven**. Indicate that they have five minutes of quiet to do with as they please. They may choose to do some writing on this page.

After the five minutes of quiet give them ten minutes to share in their groups on the reflections, celebrations, new insights, intentions, etc.

Step 12 • 5 minutes   Purpose #2, #3, #4

Announce the Time and Place of the Next Meeting

Suggest that the elders review at home **Items Five** through **Ten** and read and reflect on the biblical texts that were used in Section I.

Have the participants form a circle.

Call the group to prayer. Indicate that you will offer a prayer from a lay elder, Mary Fugate, after which anyone who wishes to pray aloud may do so. After those prayers have been offered you will close.

Begin the prayers with this prayer:

Shepherd of Israel, the source of hope and life eternal, we thank you for the rich heritage that is ours through the elders of the early church. Their love, strength, and faithfulness to you and the community of believers are examples for us to follow.

Father, bless this group, be with us and bring us in a closer relationship with you. Be with us together again to learn more of you and what you would have us do. As we leave this place, let us go forth to serve. In his name we pray. Amen.

Mary Fugate

NOTE: This section takes two hours with no break. It is advisable to allow two and one-half hours so that you can enjoy a break and will not feel as cramped for time. After Step 7 may be a good fifteen-minute break period. Some groups will not complete this section in one session.

Eldership in the Disciples Tradition

Purposes for Section II
1. To foster elders and their congregations in becoming communities of ministry
2. To help learners to be formed spiritually and claim identity from historical rootage of the eldership
3. To help learners perceive eldership as a ministry with flexibility
4. To encourage communication and support in ministry among clergy, diaconate, and eldership
5. To offer ways to have elders enrich their life of prayer

Materials
1. CD player
2. *Eldership Voices* CD with **Voice Impression 5** cued
3. Extra copies of *Disciples Eldership*
4. Pencils
5. Chalkboard and chalk or flipchart, markers, and masking tape
6. Newsprint sheet from last session on functions of eldership
7. Notes for mini-lecture in Step 5
8. Prepared newsprint sheet for Step 7, "Assessment of Eldership"
9. Pocket calculator

Steps in Section II

Step 1 • 15 minutes   Purposes #1, #5
Gathering
Cluster participants into groups of four. Suggest that the groups be different from those of last session. (If there are six or fewer total participants have only one group.) Welcome by name those who are attending their first session.

Begin this section by playing **Voice Impression 5**, "An Influential Elder." After playing the CD you may want to identify that this session will be looking more closely at the eldership in Disciples tradition.

Continue helping participants focus on heritage by telling them they have one minute of quiet reflection on personal history:

Name an elder or one person from your past who was a major influence on your becoming a believer in Christ or growing up as a believer in Christ and a participant in church. What were the ways that person influenced you?

After the moment of quiet, tell the people that they are to share from their reflections. Announce the rule for sharing: "Share only what you would enjoy sharing. If you have nothing you wish to share, don't hesitate to pass."

Give the groups ten minutes for sharing and tell them you will notify them after nine minutes.

Have the participants turn to **Item Twelve**. Instruct them to write the name of the person of their reflection on the blank line in the last line of the litany at the top of the page.

Lead a unison reading of the scripture and prayer in **Item Twelve**.

Step 2 • 5 minutes   Purpose #1
Course and Section Purposes
Review the course outline and purposes by having participants silently read **Item Two** and **Item Three**.

Next, have participants find **Item Thirteen**. Read aloud or briefly talk through the purposes for Section II.

Step 3 • 5 minutes   Purpose #2
Review
Two options are available for review.
1. Display the newsprint used last session to talk through the functions of eldership.

```
Functions of the Eldership
1. Teachers
2. Shepherds
3. Overseers
```

2. Go back to **Item Eleven** to have participants read their own comments from Section I.

Step 4 • 30 minutes   Purpose #2

Eldership in the Early Church and in the Reformation

Introduce the notion that who we are and what we do is influenced by our forebears. Illustrate this idea with some family custom that has passed through several generations.

Each person in the group is to number off "1–2, 1–2," etc. Number "ones" are to read **Item Fourteen** and fill in the blanks at the end of the item. Number "twos" are to do the same for **Item Fifteen**.

After ten minutes have a "one" read through his or her section with the blanks filled in so that the "twos" can write in the answers on **Item Fourteen**. Then a "two" will read that section for the "ones" to fill in their answers on **Item Fifteen**. The two readers are to read for the whole group and not just their small group. Give both the "one" and the "two" readers about five minutes to read their sections and take any questions.

Use the section below to check answers during the reading.

Item Fourteen (with answers)

Soon after the time recorded in scripture the church moved from more spontaneous, free-wheeling ministries toward structures with more *discipline* and *order*. From Ignatius we learn of *bishops* who functioned to perpetuate the faith among the elders, deacons, and people.

In other situations bishops and deacons were elected and served in each *congregation*.

The pattern that gained dominance in the second and third centuries was of a bishop with oversight of a *diocese* who was seen as being from an unbroken line of successors back to the apostles. *Elders* emerged as priests. Thus, in this three-fold ministry of *bishop, priest,* and *deacon* a separate clerical order came into the life of the church.

The idea of *lay elder*, however, did not completely disappear. Some men and women became *hermits* who went to the desert for solitude, silence, and prayer. They returned or were sought out to give spiritual *guidance*.

Item Fifteen (with answers)

Martin Luther appealed to princes and city magistrates—laypersons—to reform the church. He argued with rough-hewn eloquence for the *priesthood* of all *believers*, asserting that any honorable vocation is religious and that all laypersons need not be dependent upon the church hierarchy for their understanding of scripture. They are saved by *faith* through the grace of Christ and not by the mediating service of the *priesthood*.

John Calvin was the reformer with the primary influence over the Church of *Scotland*, the church of origin for three founders of the Christian Church (Disciples of Christ). Calvin argued for a four-fold ministry of *elders* (preaching, teaching, and ruling) and deacons.

The teaching of the Church of Scotland fostered lay elders. They, with the *pastor*, celebrated the Lord's supper each Lord's Day, served as *teachers,* and *counseled* the members in matters of faith and morals.

Step 5 • 5 minutes   Purpose #2
Alexander Campbell's Teaching on Ministry

You will give a mini-lecture using information below. Inform participants that they can find an outline of your remarks in **Item Sixteen.**

In 1839 Alexander Campbell, one of the founders of the Christian Church (Disciples of Christ), helped his followers clarify the issue of ministry. He very practically realized functions had to be assigned if the church was to get its work done. "Whatever is every person's business is no person's business."

He said that the ministry of Christ's church has three and only three orders: (from *Christian System*—1839)

CAMPBELL'S THREE ORDERS OF MINISTRY

1. *Evangelists*   2. *Deacons*   3. *Elders* (or bishops)

Note that Campbell has no clergy. He warned against making the church a "kingdom of the clergy." He gleefully deflated "hireling priests," especially the proud graduates of theological seminaries.

While many Disciples clergy today do not enjoy Campbell's taunts against the clergy, they do share with Campbell the dislike of dividing the church into the categories of clergy and laity. They share with him the belief that the ministry is Christ's ministry and the practice and perpetuation of the faith is seated in the congregation—not in special people set apart.

1. Evangelists

   Evangelists were ministers on the move, establishing congregations. Their work was directed primarily toward those who were outside the family of faith—not to the church people.

   When the evangelist had done his work, a congregation was formed and it elected mature males of righteous character to be leaders. These leaders were not ministers by occupation; they were farmers, shopkeepers, or teachers.

2. Deacons

   Deacons, according to Campbell, had quite varied duties, including but not limited to the "temporal interests of the community." Apparently this meant care of church property, supervision of the collection of the offering and its distribution to the poor, and ministry to the sick.

   Deacons (and the term is now often used for both men and women) are in a ministry of humility. "The first shall be last, but the last shall be first."[23]

---

[23] Ronald E. Osborn, p. 79, and *One Diaconate,* ed. by Peter Morgan. Christian Board of Publication, 1977.

3. Elders

This course will concentrate primarily on the other order of ministry named by Campbell—the eldership. As Campbell said: Their duty is "to preside over, to instruct, and to edify the community—to feed the church of the Lord with knowledge and understanding. To watch for their souls, as those that must give account to the Lord." [24]

The eldership for Disciples has the three functions that we studied in Section I:

1. Teachers

2. Shepherds

3. Overseers

Ronald Osborn summarizes our tradition of the eldership. "The office of ministry in a Christian congregation rested primarily in the eldership, a select body of upright men ordained to preside over the life of the church, to exercise pastoral oversight, to teach the word of God, to maintain discipline, to minister at the table, to set an example to the flock. In a given congregation most, if not all, of the men earned their living at secular vocations. But they were appointed to minister in the church of God." [25]

Step 6 • 5 minutes   Purposes #2, #3

Profile of a Disciples Elder of 1850

Play **Voice Impression 6**, using an introduction in your own words.

Sample introduction:
Listen to Peter Morgan describe an elder from 1850. He will recite part of Vachel Lindsay's poem "The Proud Farmer." You will have a copy of the poem in Item Seventeen.

Step 7 • 15 minutes   Purpose #3

Assessment of Eldership

The groups are now to assess how much the elders of their congregations are doing to fulfill the traditional functions of eldership. They will use **Item Eighteen** as a way to begin dialogue on how much "eldering" is being done.

Instruct the groups to select a tabulator. Then they are to fill in **Item Eighteen** without discussion. Remind them to assess quantity, not quality. Each person is to report to the tabulator his or her score on the three categories. Have them hold discussion until after the tabulator gets the group averages. The tabulators are then to come forward and use magic markers to fill in the newsprint that you have prepared prior to the session.

Discussion in the groups on reasons behind assessments begins when the tabulator leaves to write the group averages.

---

[24] Alexander Campbell, *Christian System*. Christian Publishing Company, 1839, p. 84.

[25] Ronald E. Osborn, "The Eldership Among the Disciples of Christ," pp. 82–84.

| Copy this chart on newsprint.

RATING OUR ELDERSHIP			
Teaching	Shepherding	Overseeing	Group Average
Group A _____	_____	_____	_____
Group B _____	_____	_____	_____
Group C _____	_____	_____	_____
Group D _____	_____	_____	_____
Total Average _____	_____	_____	_____

While groups continue their discussion, you are to figure the total average for each of the three functions:
Teaching
Shepherding
Overseeing
A pocket calculator will be helpful.

After the discussions, go over the chart with the entire group. First, indicate that this process is not guaranteed to give an accurate picture of your congregation's eldership. It is meant to open the discussion on how much of the traditional eldership functions the eldership is currently doing.

Next, point out high and low group averages. Indicate how the total averages compare. Which is high? Which is low? Is the overall average generally high, low, or middle?

Step 8 • 10 minutes   Purposes #2, #3, #4
Mini-lecture on the Odyssey of Disciples
Now have the group listen closely to a mini-lecture by Peter Morgan as he highlights the odyssey of *Disciples Eldership*. Play **Voice Impression 7**, and encourage the participants to take notes for their later personal review. Leaders may develop their own mini-lecture from the material in **Item Twenty**.

Step 9 • 15 minutes   Purpose #2
Reflections on Section II
Give your groups some time to absorb, integrate, challenge, appreciate (whatever they wish to do) all the material they have covered in Section II. Have them turn to **Item Nineteen**. Indicate that they have five minutes of quiet to do with as they please. They may choose to do some writing on this page.

After the five minutes of quiet, give them ten minutes to share in their groups on their reflections, celebrations, new intentions, etc.

Assignment and Closing Prayer

Announce the time and place of the next meeting. Give assignment. Offer closing prayers.

The assignment is to read, before the next session, Dr. Richard Pope's paper on "The Elder in Disciples History," **Item Twenty**. Indicate that the next session will begin the section of the course on the elders' function in ministry.

Have the participants form a circle in which each one is standing close to others.

Call the group to prayer. Indicate that you will offer a prayer from Bill Mitchell, an elder, after which anyone who wishes to pray aloud may do so. After those prayers have been offered you will close.

Begin the prayers with this prayer:

Our Father, it would be very easy to be simply overwhelmed by the many facets of being elders that have been opened to us.

But rather than be discouraged, we choose to be challenged by the many opportunities, and thank you for them.

You may not expect us to be a modern day Alexander Campbell, Martin Luther, or John Calvin. We pray, Father, that we may have the courage to make the most of our special talents and, with your support and the encouragement of our fellow Christians, we pray that we may meet or exceed your expectations for us.

We pray that our efforts may be fruitful in pointing the way for others to experience for themselves the inner strength and peace of mind that comes from willing obedience to our savior, Jesus Christ, in whose name we pray. Amen.
        Bill Mitchell

NOTE: This section takes two hours with no break. It is advisable to allow two and one-half hours so that you will not feel as cramped for time. After Step 6 may be a good fifteen-minute break period. Some groups will not complete this section in one session.

S E C T I O N   I I I

As Elders Teach

Purposes for Section III
1. To foster elders and their congregations in becoming communities of ministry
2. To help learners perceive and practice eldership as a ministry with flexibility
3. To enable learners to provide knowledgeable and effective ministry as **teachers**
4. To offer ways to enrich the life of prayer of individuals and groups
5. To offer guidance for the ongoing life of the eldership

Materials
1. Copies of denominational and regional newsletters/magazine.
2. Newsprint and markers for each group
3. Masking tape
4. Extra copies of *Disciples Eldership*
5. Extra pencils
6. CD player
7. *Eldership Voices* CD with **Voice Impression 8** cued

Steps in Section III

Step 1 • 3 minutes   Purpose #1

Suggested Introductory Comments:

Sections I and II of this course helped our eldership to be spiritually formed by our scriptural and traditional identity. The course now moves from a quest for identity to a quest for effective ministry. Sections III through VI will help us live out our effective ministry.

The interplay between spiritual formation and action will be evident in the next four sections. For example, in Sections I and II we discovered that part of our identity as an eldership is to be teachers.

In today's session we want an action plan of ministry as teachers to emerge out of our biblical and historical identity as teachers.

Find **Item Twenty-One** *in your resource and we will read aloud the purposes for Section III.*

As we begin thinking about the elders' ministry of teaching, let us listen to Richard Pope talk about being a teaching elder.

Play **Voice Impression 8.**

A good way to present the purposes in this and the remaining sections is to print **Item Twenty-One** on newsprint. Underline "teachers" in Purpose Three. In Sections IV through VI use this same newsprint and insert in Purpose Three, "shepherds," "celebrators of the Lord's supper," or "overseers."

Another option for moving into this section is to have comments from those who read **Item Twenty** at home. Then begin your remarks with paragraph two of the suggested introductory comments (above).

Step 2 • 5 minutes   Purpose #4

Identity as Teachers Recalled and Expanded

Have participants individually review the biblical material on teaching in **Item Seven** and some of their own reflections and discussions in **Item Eighteen**.

To help expand elders' ideas of the teaching ministry play **Voice Impression 9,** Robert Glover on biblical elder as tribal leader. Bob is an elder and a leading Christian educator.

Step 3 • 2 minutes   Purposes #1, #3
(Step 3, Step 4, or Step 6 may be omitted to save time.)

Section Overview

Give the participants a "cognitive map" for this session. Write on newsprint, "The eldership is a <u>community</u> of <u>teaching</u> and <u>learning</u>." Explain that this section is organized around those three underlined terms. First, community will be experienced. Second, you'll explore, "How does eldership fulfill its teaching ministry, especially since not all elders necessarily should be in a classroom?" Third, ideas will be generated for elders as learners.

Step 4 • 10 minutes   Purpose #1

Gathering the Community of Teachers/Learners

Have participants form groups of four. Encourage each person to be part of a group that has at least one person who was not in his or her small group in the first two sections.

After the groups are seated, have them take thirty seconds to select a recorder to be used later.

The groups are to reflect in silence on "My most valuable discovery or experience in the last twelve months." Have them note their reflections in Item Twenty-Two. They are to work both on their experience or insight and theological reflections during the quiet time. Allow three minutes for this task.

Let the people share in the small groups their stories, discoveries, and the related theological reflections. Let them know that they have five minutes for sharing. Notify them when one minute remains.

Conclude this step by labeling, or "naming," the activity just finished. You may use the sample leader comment below.

Enrichment often comes to us when we speak of our experiences and thoughts and others listen to us carefully. The enrichment goes both ways. Enrichment comes to us when we love people enough to listen carefully.

Let me label what we have been doing.

First, we have been <u>teaching</u> each other. Sharing of experiences and reflections to enrich others is one kind of teaching.

Second, we have been <u>building a community of growth and enrichment</u>. Our faith is enlivened and enlightened as God becomes present to us through a community of growing, searching, listening Christians.

Use chalkboard or newsprint to write the following:

1. teaching

2. building a community of growth and enrichment

Prayer

Instruct the groups to stand in a circle with shoulders touching. Have them place their hands together in the center of the circle.

Lead them with the following prayer:

Eternal and most loving God: You have called us into being both as persons and as a group. You have opened to us the mysteries of your creation and have given us sight, hearing, and reason that we might know the meaning of existence. You have given us understanding of good and evil, light and darkness, and freedom that we might choose between right and wrong. You have taught us to live in love and mutual helpfulness. We have received the gifts of scripture and the record of your working within the church and in all of history. We have received the gift of your Son in whom all knowledge and understanding reside and in whom we experience the ultimate meaning of life and death.

For these gifts we lift our hearts in praise and thanksgiving.

In these quiet moments together, help us to understand that as we have received, so also must we give. We have been given tongues to speak, words and symbols through which we may communicate the knowledge we have received from you. We have been given hands to reach out and touch in the loving ministry of teaching.

Dear God, give us clear vision, sound hearing, and correct understanding, that through our speaking and our living we may faithfully interpret your will for us and for all your people. Amen.
Virginia Liggett

The Eldership Is a Teaching/Learning Community

Step 6 is to help continue to build the participants into a community.

Tell participants that you are going to give them one minute to ponder in silence a question. Then they will have four minutes to share with each other from their reflections.

The question: "What do you need in words and deeds from a group for you to know that you belong with them?"

As the sharing begins, advise the groups to listen carefully to each person. "You are receiving vital information for continuing to grow into a caring community."

Step 7 • 27 minutes   Purposes #2, #3

A Community of Teaching/Learning

The emphasis in this step is on community.

Have everyone turn to **Item Twenty-Three.** Very briefly go through the steps: reading, silence, writing, and sharing. Indicate that they will have fifteen minutes for reading **Item Twenty-Four,** silence, and writing. You will signal them at the end of five minutes and ten minutes. At the end of fifteen minutes have each group share from its reflections and writings. The sharing is to last for ten minutes. The recorder is to take down recommendations to be reported later in the session, and to write those recommendations in magic marker on newsprint for presentation in Step 10. The recorder will also make reports from the same newsprint sheets on recommendations from Steps 8 and 9.

Step 8 • 33 minutes   Purposes #2, #3

Elders as Teachers

How do elders fulfill their teaching ministry? Earlier in the session we heard Bob Glover speak of the biblical elder as not only an officer but as a wisdom figure of the tribe, the family. Play **Voice Impression 10** in which Bob tells of Buffy Saint-Marie's article on Indian elders teaching their tribal lore to the children. Give your groups five minutes to discuss the following two topics. You may want to put these on newsprint before the session.

1. In your lifetime have you experienced an elder passing along the lore of the "Christian tribe," the church?

2. What traits or gifts are important to cultivate as one of the "storytellers" who lead the church?

Have your groups listen to another comment by Bob Glover, this time as it applies to the elders' teaching in the church today, **Voice Impression 11.** Suggest that the participants write down ideas from Bob, which they may want to remember later when they will be sharing recommendations for the future ministry of teaching by elders.

"Contributors to the Growing Wisdom and Knowledge of the Congregation," **Item Twenty-Six,** is another resource for stimulating ideas on how your elders may grow in faithfulness as teachers.

Before the reading, talk through the steps in **Item Twenty-Five,** which is a tool for reflection and building of recommendations. Allow ten minutes for reading, silence, and writing. Let participants know when to begin the ten-minute sharing period. The recorder is to write down recommendations for use near the end of the session.

Step 9 • 20 minutes   Purposes #2, #3

Elders as Learners

The eldership is a community of learners who reach out to teach the congregation in formal and informal ways. **Item Twenty-Eight** is for use in generating ideas in ways elders can be a community of growth. **Item Twenty-Seven** is the worksheet that participants are to review before reading **Item Twenty-Eight.**

The reading assignment is to be divided among the participants. Have the participants number off, with "3" being the highest number. The "ones" are to find the selection on "Bible Study" in **Item Twenty-Eight,** the "twos" are to find two selections, "Worship Leaders and Shepherds" and "Identity with the Larger Church," and the "threes" are to find "Ideas for Faithful Mission." The objective here is for each participant to read the assignment, reflect on it, and contribute ideas toward making the eldership a community of learners. The recorder will again be busy during the sharing. You as leader will keep time. Give ten minutes for reading, silence, and writing. The small group discussion time will take five minutes.

Step 10 • 4 minutes   Purpose #5

Recommendations

Have each recorder briefly read through his or her group's recommendations from **Items Twenty-Three, Twenty-Five,** and **Twenty-Seven.**

Before next session combine and compile all these recommendations onto one newsprint sheet. *You will produce one of these sheets for each of Sections III, IV, V, and VI for use in formulating your plan for eldership in Section VI.* Keep these emerging ideas before the study group by displaying them in each session.

Step 11 • 1 minute   Purposes #2, #3

Assignment

Next section will be on "As Elders Shepherd." The assignment before the next section is to reread **Items Twenty-Four, Twenty-Six,** and **Twenty-Eight.**

Step 12 • 4 minutes   Purpose #4

Closing Worship

Call everyone into a time of prayer. Give two or three minutes for persons to offer comments. Allow them to be free to lift up concerns, frustrations, and fatigue, as well as thanksgiving and celebrations for points of growth.

Conclude with the following prayer from elder Virginia Liggett.

Eternal and most gracious God:

We stand before you and in the presence of these your servants, grateful that you have brought us to this moment in the pilgrimage of our faith. From the first stirrings of belief and confidence, through periods of doubt and disillusionment, to growing maturity and deepened commitment, we have been aware of your leading as our faith has been nurtured by so great a host of parents, teachers, deacons, elders, and pastors. We have seen you at work in them as they have opened the meaning of scripture, the history of your redeeming action in the lives of people and nations, the spread of the gospel to every corner of the world, the relevance of your Word for life today and hope for the future.

In this solemn moment we affirm the gifts we have received from you and we accept our teaching ministry with gratitude and joy. We commit ourselves to study, both alone and in this group, opening ourselves in silence to the leading of your Spirit, that our teaching may speak of faithfulness, integrity, encouragement, confidence, and joy. We will seek to recognize, understand, and respond to the potential for learning, the search for meaning, the particular needs, and the longing for relationship of every child, youth, and adult both within this congregation and outside for whom the church exists.

Endow us, O God, with diligence, strength, courage, and above all with self-giving love as we seek to be faithful in our learning and in our teaching. Amen.
Virginia Liggett

NOTE: This section takes two hours with no break. It is advisable to allow two and one-half hours so that you will not feel as cramped for time. After Step 7 may be a good fifteen-minute break period. Some groups will not complete this section in one session.

As Elders Shepherd

Purposes for Section IV
1. To foster elders and their congregations in becoming communities of ministry
2. To help learners perceive and practice eldership as a ministry with flexibility
3. To enable learners to provide knowledgeable and effective ministry as shepherds
4. To offer ways to enrich the life of prayer of individuals and groups
5. To offer guidance for the ongoing life of the eldership

Materials
1. CD player
2. *Eldership Voices* CD with **Voice Impression 12** cued
3. Pencils
4. Flipchart, markers, and masking tape
5. Newsprint prepared ahead of session with two sheets described in Step 6
6. Character description cards for each group (see Step 6)

Steps in Section IV

Step 1 • 7 minutes   Purpose #1

Gathering

Allow a few moments for people to catch up on the news of what has been happening in their lives since the last session. Again you may want to have chairs arranged by fours. Take a few seconds to arrange the groups into four persons each.

Announce that the section is on "As Elders Shepherd." To get to the specific purposes for this section have the groups find **Item Twenty-Nine** in the resource book. The individuals in each group are to "letter off," A, B, C, or D. Each person takes one purpose (person A takes purpose 1, person B takes purpose 2, etc., omit purpose 5), reads it silently, writes the purpose in his or her own words, and jots down a couple of ideas on how the fulfillment of that purpose can change the congregation. Give the groups five minutes to share the purposes in their own words and their ideas on that purpose's possible impact on the congregation. Remember that this is a warm-up, so don't allow the discussions to carry over into time the groups will need for other learning activities.

Step 2 • 5 minutes   Purposes #1, #3

Our Identity as Shepherds

Sample comment:

Our actions are determined by our thoughts about ourselves. If, for example, we have been claimed by a vision of ourselves as being shepherds who will help bring God's love to others, that's the way we will act.

Before we get to the issues of how we fulfill a ministry as shepherds, let us review our heritage as elders, which seeks to claim us. Find **Items Eight, Sixteen,** *and the discussion in* **Eighteen** *and absorb some of the message that we are called to live out. Take three or four minutes with the review.*

Step 3 • 15 minutes   Purposes #1, #2, #3

Images by which Elderships Grow in Self-Understanding

This training on elders as shepherds seeks to cultivate in the eldership of the Christian Church (Disciples of Christ) a few special gifts that come very easily and naturally to some elders, but only with patience and practice for others.

What are some of these special gifts? **Voice Impression 12,** "Shepherding Elders," has three persons relating their personal experiences with gifted, shepherding elders. Play this voice impression to your group members, suggesting they note those special qualities of elders being highlighted on the CD.

After listening to the voice impression, list on the chalkboard/flipchart those special qualities noted by the participants.

Lead into a brief, total group sharing on well-loved elders from the past in your congregation.

Sample Comment:

Most congregations have had elders with unique shepherding gifts. Who would you name as that well-loving, shepherding elder who has served or is serving our congregation?

What characteristics do you appreciate about that elder?

Allow a couple of minutes for this sharing.

Introduce the study of images of eldership.

Sample Comment:

Images, or word pictures, can enlighten our ideas on what an elder is and what an elder does. We studied one word picture in the Bible in Section I. To review, look at **Item Thirty**. *Let's read together 1 Peter 5:1–4.*

"Shepherd" is our first word picture. In **Item Thirty** *and* **Voice Impression 13** *you can read and hear two other word pictures of eldership and hear a poignant example of the first of these word pictures.*

First play **Voice Impression 13**, and then have the group take five minutes for reading **Item Thirty**. After listening and reading have participants discuss the images in their small groups, asking them to share the names of people in their congregation who have the traits described by these images.

Step 4 • 5 minutes   Purposes #1, #4

Prayer

You will lead the prayer below, which uses the power to visualize.

Sample Comment:

Jewish mothers, and gatekeepers, these images teach us that elders pay attention to people in a caring way.

Prayer both intensifies our attention to the people for whom we pray and it is one way of caring.

As we prepare for prayer, I am going to ask you to relax, to be aware of your body, to locate points of stress in your body, and relax those points of stress. Soon you will close your eyes and I will suggest people for you to picture. Use the backs of your eyelids as a screen to look at the people who come to mind. Close your eyes.

Read the first suggestion below and then wait for thirty seconds before quietly offering the next suggestion. Wait thirty seconds between each suggestion and close with the prayer at the end of the list.

- Picture a person who appreciates your congregation very deeply.
  (Thirty seconds of silence)

- Picture a person who is upset with the church now or someone who doesn't attend as often as he or she used to.
  (Thirty seconds of silence)

- Picture a member who never attends.
  (Thirty seconds of silence)

- Picture a new member.
  (Thirty seconds of silence)

- Picture a shut-in.
  (Thirty seconds of silence)

Offer the following prayer:

My beloved God,

I praise and glorify you in this hour, and I thank you for having called me into your service, and above all for allowing me to serve my brothers and sisters and to share with them that which by grace I have received from you.

Lord, I am very limited, but I ask you to be glorified in my limitations. Help me to serve…only to serve. Fill my hands each day so that, without any prejudice, I may pour your gifts over my brothers and sisters.

Lord, I confess that at times I feel weak and tired; for example when I start to trust my own strength or at those times when I am misunderstood. But I know that you are always alert to my needs and ready to provide me with new strengths.

Thank you again, my dear Lord. In the name of Jesus I pray, Amen.
Irma Diaz

(The original Spanish version is provided below.)

Mi querido Dios,

Yo te alabo y te glorifico en esta hora, y te doy gracias por haberme llamado a tu servicio; sobre todo, por permitirme servirle a mis hermanos y compartir con ellos, lo que por gracia he recibido de ti.

Señor, soy muy limitada, pero te pido que te glorifiues en mi limitación. Ayúdame a servir y solamente a servir. Llena mis manos cada día para vertirlas sobre mis hermanos sin hacer diferencias.

Señor, te confieso que a veces me siento débil y cansada; especialmente curando empiezo a confiar en mis propias fuerzas, o cuando me siento incomprendida. Pero you se que tu siempre estas atento a mi necesidad, y dispuesto a darme nuevas fuerzas.

Gracias, mi buen Dios. En el nombre de Jesús te lo pido, Amen.

Step 5 • 20 minutes   Purpose #3

Different Levels of Participation

A mini-lecture will help your participants to identify various levels of participation and to begin picturing individuals in each of those levels. An essential for shepherding is knowing people and their needs.

You have a couple of options in preparing for the mini-lecture. The easiest way is to listen to **Voice Impression 14** and decide to use it as it is in the session. Another option is for you to become so familiar with the CD lecture and the material in **Item Thirty-One** in the resource book that it can be given as your own lecture.

Before you begin the lecture in the session have participants find **Item Thirty-One**. They are to follow the material on the page during the course of the lecture. After the first part of the lecture, the participants will work on the first three columns of the item. They may follow the rest of the lecture in the last column as they hear it. Give the groups a few minutes to share reactions to the lecture and some of the names that came to mind for each of the categories.

Step 6 • 45 minutes   Purpose #3

Sample Training

The training to be experienced by your groups is a sample. The hope is that some knowledge and skills will be acquired in this sample on a shepherd's care of new members. Primarily, however, the sample is to help with the decision of whether or not to have this kind of training in shepherding skills beyond this course.

You are offering a first lick to see if they wish to buy the ice cream cone.

Begin by having people remember the letter they chose in Step 1— A, B, C, or D.

Next, put this sample comment into your own words.

Much of our learning, like bike riding, comes only by practice. This sample training is to help us learn to be shepherds of new members. We are going to practice on each other. You would be uncomfortable for your dentist to have never practiced before he or she worked on you. What about those new families trying to find their way into becoming known and loved and engaged in ministry in our congregation? They deserve for us to practice before we go out to be their shepherds.

Instructions for the Leader

As you now move into the actual training, you will need:

1. Box I and Box II on newsprint or chalkboard (see below)

2. Typed or printed character descriptions on 3x5 cards (those playing new members B-C in round one will receive an identical character card)

A couple of samples you may use are printed below. You may also use descriptions of persons who have joined your congregations within the last year. Of course, do not disclose confidential information about any person being portrayed.

New Members

A newly married couple just moved to town

Husband—You are in your first job out of college, an engineer. You joined the church primarily to please your wife. You have little experience in the church and no previous church membership.

Wife—You are a teacher looking for work. You are deeply religious and you have always been part of the church even though your family moved frequently. As a young teenager you were part of a Disciples congregation for two years.

New Members

Forty-five-year-old couple

She owns and manages a hardware store. He is a salesperson in a florist shop. This couple has two sons. One is a sophomore in college. The other is married and is a long-distance trucker.

Two years ago the couple nearly divorced. In a new resolve to save the marriage they decided to join the church. No one at church knows about the marital problem except the pastor.

She dominates the relationship.

Slowly and carefully talk through the material you have prepared ahead of time on the newsprint so that everyone understands the procedure.

BOX I	
Round 1	
Person A—You are an elder	Be yourself
Persons B and C— You are a new member	The specifics of your character are on the card you get from the leaders
Person D— You are an observer	You will have a form to use
(Round 1 has three phases)	
Round 2	
Person A— You are a new member	The specifics of your character are on the card you get from the leaders
Person B—You are an elder	Be yourself
Person C— You are an observer	You will have a form to use
Person D— You are a new member	The specifics of your character are on the card you get from the leaders
(Round 2 has three phases)	

```
┌──────────────────────────────────────────────────────────────┐
│                          BOX II                                │
│  Phase 1—(five minutes)                                        │
│  Preparation                                                   │
│     Elders—          Read Item Thirty-Two and plan the call    │
│     Observers—       Read Item Thirty-Two (elder's material) and│
│                      become familiar with Item Thirty-Three for│
│                      your use during the call and the discussion│
│                      following                                 │
│     New                                                        │
│     Members—         Study character cards and visit with each other│
│                      about the role                            │
│                                                                │
│  Phase 2—(ten minutes)                                         │
│     The call                                                   │
│                                                                │
│  Phase 3—(five minutes)                                        │
│     Both "elders" and "new members" are to participate after  │
│     observer's first comments. The observer offers comments and│
│     leads discussion.                                          │
└──────────────────────────────────────────────────────────────┘
```

Keep it light. This kind of learning is to be fun. Also, be alert for notifying people of the time to change activities, and to move from Round 1 to Round 2.

Step 7 • 20 minutes   Purpose #5

Build Recommendations List

As you prepare to lead this step you may need to review the procedure for formulating recommendations, Steps 7 and 10 of Section III.

Begin Step 7 with a rhetorical question. "What form of our shepherding ministry do you wish to emerge out of your study and prayer and experiences?"

Two specific ideas are to be considered: first, a shepherding plan, Item Thirty-Five, and second, training in shepherding in the style just experienced in the sample on shepherding new members. In addition, encourage the participants to be open to God's spirit as they cultivate their own ideas as they use Item Thirty-Four.

The reading of Item Thirty-Five is to take five minutes, the silence two minutes, the writing three minutes, and the sharing five minutes. Person "D" is to be appointed recorder before the sharing begins.

At the conclusion of the sharing the group recorders are to report to the larger group.

Keep copies of these reports for use in deciding the future of ministry of your eldership in Section VI.

Step 8 • 3 minutes   Purpose #4

Closing the Session

Announce the assignment: The participants are to read all of **Item Thirty** again.

Part of shepherding is a ministry of prayer for those persons under one's care.

Invite any one who wishes to participate to say,
"I pray for _____ (name)."

The entire group will join that person's prayer by saying
"We pray for _____ (name)."

NOTE: This section takes two hours with no break. It is advisable to allow two and one-half hours so that you will not feel cramped for time. After Step 5 may be a good fifteen-minute break period. Some groups will not complete this section in one session.

As Elders Celebrate the Lord's Supper

Purposes for Section V

1. To foster elders and their congregations in becoming communities of ministry

2. To help learners perceive and practice eldership as a ministry with flexibility

3. To enable learners to provide knowledgeable and effective ministry as celebrants of the Lord's supper

4. To offer ways to enrich the life of prayer of individuals and groups

5. To offer guidance for the ongoing life of the eldership

Materials

1. CD player

2. *Eldership Voices* CD with **Voice Impression 15** cued

3. Pencils

4. Flipchart, markers, and masking tape

Steps in Section V

Step 1 • 8 minutes   Purpose #1
Gathering
Catch up on what's been happening with the members of the study group by having them think about and share, "the most interesting or important happening in my life since our last session." If your group is small enough to complete this catching up in five minutes, share as a total group. If not, have them share in groups of four.

The last three minutes of this step are for reading **Item Thirty-Six**. Note key ideas gained since the study began, or identify events in the congregation that reflect the purposes. You may wish to use the newsprint copy of the purposes and write in "celebrants of the Lord's supper" in Purpose Three. Participants are to be in groups of four by the completion of this step.

Step 2 • 15 minutes   Purposes #2, #3
A New Term: Folk Priest
The term "folk priest" is not introduced in order to become a widely used label for the Disciples lay elder. The term is to help congregations and elders deepen their understanding of what elders do when they serve at the Lord's Table. Open the subject by playing **Voice Impression 15**, "Folk Priests."

Assign the study paper on folk priests, **Item Thirty-Seven**, for reading and discussion. Five minutes have been allotted for reading, seven for discussion.

Step 3 • 18 minutes   Purposes #2, #3
Knowledge of Worship and Knowledge of the Lord's Supper
Two reading assignments will be given to two different sets of readers. Each group is to take ten seconds to select two "A" persons and two "B" persons. "A's" are to read **Item Thirty-Eight** and be prepared to share their learnings on "Worship" with "B's." "B's" are to read **Item Thirty-Nine** and be prepared to share their learnings on "The Lord's Supper" with "A's."

"A's" and "B's" are to take eight minutes to read their assignments at the same time.

As leader you want to master to content of both **Items Thirty Eight** and **Thirty-Nine**.

During the "share your learnings," work as a total group to state the information in **Item Thirty-Eight**. Suggest to "B's" that they take notes (space at end of **Item Thirty-Eight**).

Make sure the "A's" include:

1. The three acts of worship

2. The use of lectionaries

3. The Christian year

4. The relationship of the service of the Word to the service of the Lord's supper

You will need to keep fairly strict enforcement of the five minute time limit or this discussion will leak beyond the limits of the purpose of the session.

Use the same procedure for total group sharing of information in **Item Thirty-Nine.** "B's" are to be a resource in helping to bring out the information contained in the item. "A's" may wish to take notes. Note taking space in margins available on pages 64–66.

Make sure the "B's" recite and briefly describe the steps in the Lord's supper:

1. Words of institution

2. The approach

3. The offering

4. Communion prayer

5. The breaking of bread and distribution

6. The conclusion

Again, keep fairly strict control over the five minutes allotted for sharing the information in **Item Thirty-Nine.** Evaluation of your congregation's practice of the Lord's supper, while important, is not to be done now. That discussion needs to be held when it won't compete with the other important work that needs to be done in this section.

Step 4 • 33 minutes   Purposes #3, #4

A Prayerful Person

Sample Comment:

The prayers at the table are the overflow of the life of prayer and meditation of the elder. Portions from a Matthew Kelty letter on the CD will lead us into an experience of prayer.

Play **Voice Impression 16.** The quiet time of solitude and prayer mentioned by Matthew Kelty is to be experienced by your participants in a prayer vigil.

Prepare ahead of the session the details of where the people are to go to be alone, when they are to return, and how they are to be signaled to return to the group. After giving these instructions have participants find **Item Forty.** Go through the steps of prayer in the middle of the paper. Point out the prayers by John Baillie at the end of the item and the space for writing to be used as they conclude the vigil. Give participants time to read silently **Item Forty** and move out to their vigil spot when they have finished reading. Participants are to have about fifteen minutes of solitude and then return to their small groups for eight minutes of sharing. As leader you will need to give simple, clear directions. Also, let participants know that you will help them by watching the time for them and calling them back together after the vigil.

Step 5 • 31 minutes   Purposes #3, #4

A Skilled Celebrant of the Lord's Supper

The participants are to learn the themes for extemporaneous communion prayers and then practice writing prayers.

Begin by listening to Paul Crow on **Voice Impression 17,** "Prayer at the Lord's Table." Dr. Crow speaks out of his experience as an elder, a former professor of church history, and a Disciple who is recognized for his ecumenical leadership. Next, have everyone find **Item Forty-One** and read it.

Allow five minutes for the reading. You may choose to have the paper summarized by small groups. To assure that the information in the study paper is clearly understood, a total group summary is preferred. With either choice four minutes is allotted for the summaries.

Item Forty-Two is a work sheet. Prayers are written out with a line given in which each participant is to write the themes of the pattern. After three minutes give the answers to see that every one understands how the pattern fits the prayer. The exercise continues with each person writing a communion prayer using the pattern and based on the scripture lesson provided. Give ten minutes for reading the lectionary selection and writing the prayer using the pattern. The remaining seven minutes is for the small groups to hear the prayers they have just written.

Step 6 • 10 minutes   Purposes #5

Recommendations and Personal Commitments

All are given five minutes for reflection and work in **Item Forty-Three**. They are to prayerfully consider the effect the learnings of this session are to have on the eldership, on the congregation, and on themselves. Those reflections are to be written as recommendations for the eldership and as statements of personal commitment.

Begin the five minute sharing period by naming a recorder in each group. *He or she will take notes on the recommendations that you will collect and later compile onto newsprint for use in Section VI.*

Step 7 • 5 minutes   Purposes #1, #2, #4

Closing and Assignments

The participants are to read all the study papers used in this session. It is very important for all persons to read the study papers not assigned to them during the session. A second assignment is to engage in daily intercession for a week. The person for whom each one prays is the one in the small group with the same letter, "A" or "B," given in Step 3. After the session, these prayer pairs may wish to visit privately about special needs and prayer requests.

Close by giving the total group one minute of silence in which each person begins the week of intercession for his or her prayer partner. Lead people out of the silence as you pray aloud the following prayer:

Lord,

God of love and mercy.

We thank you for being able to pray..., for being able to use that effective means of communication with you. We thank you for the unity that we have experienced by praying together, and for the assurance of having been heard by you.

I ask you, O God, that this renewing experience of prayer be converted into bread of eternal life in our soul, and that many others will benefit themselves through our life of prayer.

Now, O Lord, give us the spiritual strength to learn to accompany our moments of solitude with your presence, through prayer.

We pray in the powerful name of Christ, Amen.

Josué Martínez

(The original Spanish version is provided below.)

Señor,

Dios de amor y misericordia, te damos gracias por la oración, por ese medio eficaz para comunicarnos contigo. Te damos gracias por la unidad que hemos experimentado orando juntos, y por la certeza de haber side oídos por ti.

Te pedimos, O Dios, que esta experiencia renovadora se traduzca en pan de Vida Eterna en nuestro ser, y que sean muchos los que se beneficien mediante nuestra vida de oración.

Ahora, Señor, danos la fortaleza espiritual para aprender a acompañar nuestros momentos de soledad con tu presencia a través de la oración.

En el nombre poderoso de Cristo, oramos, Amén.

NOTE: This section takes two hours with no break. It is advisable to allow two and one-half hours so that you will not feel cramped for time. After Step 4 may be a good fifteen-minute break period. Some groups will not complete this section in one session.

As Elders Oversee

Purposes for Section VI
1. To foster elders and their congregations in becoming communities of ministry
2. To help learners perceive and practice eldership as a ministry with flexibility
3. To enable learners to provide knowledgeable and effective ministry as overseers
4. To offer ways to enrich the life of prayer of individuals and groups
5. To offer guidance for the ongoing life of the eldership

Materials
1. CD player
2. *Eldership Voices* CD with **Voice Impression 18** cued
3. Pencils
4. Flipchart, markers, and masking tape
5. Calculator
6. Newsprint, recommendations from Sections III, IV, V

Steps in Section VI

Step 1 • 5 minutes   Purpose #1

Gathering

Have the room set up in sets of four chairs in circles. Let this room arrangement determine the small groups by letting those who sit together work together. Each group will need to take a few seconds to select a recorder. Have participants find **Item Forty-Four**, which contains the purposes for the section. Give them one minute to read the purposes silently.

You as leader may wish to add the word "overseers" to Purpose Three on the newsprint copy and point it out to the participants.

Step 2 • 2 minutes   Purpose #4

Prayer

Call the people to prayer as they begin this section's quest to be effective overseers and as they plan for the future of the eldership of the congregation. Use the following prayer:

> Heavenly Father, as we face this new experience, help us keep our faith and trust in your power and love. Strengthen us and give us inner peace. Help us to give ourselves fully into your hands that you can give yourself to us. Take from us any uneasiness or anxiety and help us understand. Through Jesus Christ we pray. Amen.
> *David Brown*

Step 3 • 5 minutes   Purpose #3

Review

Review the eldership's identity by having participants go back to their work in Sections I and II. Give them a couple of minutes to look over their notes in **Items Nine** and **Eighteen**. You may want to give a summary statement, which can be prepared from the material in the first paragraph of **Item Forty-Five**.

An optional review step is to replay **Voice Impression 3** and recall the learnings from Step 9 in Section I.

Step 4 • 25 minutes   Purposes #2, #3

Elders Oversee

What does it mean to refer to an elder as an overseer? Play **Voice Impression 18** as you begin to identify this important aspect of the eldership. Following the voice impression have the group members briefly share what they understand it to mean to refer to the elder as overseer.

You may wish to review the procedure of reading, silence, writing, and sharing. If so, look up **Item Twenty-Three** and Step 7 of Section III.

Participants will be using **Item Forty-Five** for their reading and **Item Forty-Six** for their work space.

Review the procedure with your groups. Remind them that the recorder is to put recommendations on newsprint during the sharing time. You will be timekeeper and will notify groups at five minute intervals.

The last five minutes of this step is for reports of recommendations by each recorder.

Step 5 • 10 minutes   Purpose #5

Recommendations—Elders Teach

Steps 5 through 8 will be for reviewing recommendations for specific ways your congregation's eldership is to serve as teachers, shepherds, folk priests, and overseers.

Display the newsprint of recommendations from Section III, "As Elders Teach." Give the participants three minutes to read the recommendations and write them in Item Forty-Seven. After three minutes the groups are to use seven minutes to discuss, to ask questions, and to assess which of these recommendations are most important.

While the discussion is in progress you need to take the recommendations given on oversight in Step 4 and make one clear, simply worded list that omits duplications. This list will be used in Step 8.

Step 6 • 10 minutes   Purpose #5

Recommendations—Elders Shepherd

Display the newsprint from Section IV on shepherding recommendations. Repeat the process used in Step 5, using Item Forty-Eight.

Step 7 • 10 minutes   Purpose #5

Recommendations—Elders Celebrate the Lord's Supper

Display the newsprint from Section V on folk priest recommendations. Use Item Forty-Nine and repeat the process used in the two previous steps.

Step 8 • 10 minutes   Purpose #5

Recommendations—Elders Oversee

Display the newsprint you just prepared, which lists recommendations for elders as overseers. Again, use the process described in Step 5, using Item Fifty.

Step 9 • 20 minutes   Purpose #5

A Plan for Future Ministry

Your groups are to build a plan for the future ministry of the eldership in their congregation.

Instruct them in the scoring system used to decide what will be done. Each person is to have 100 points for use in supporting individual recommendations.

They will spend no more than 100 total points, with a maximum of 35 being spent on any topic. A person using 35 points in the first category would only have 65 remaining for use in the other three categories.

For example, one person may total 35 points spent under recommendations for teaching, 25 for shepherding, 20 for folk priest, and 20 for oversight. The total is 100.

An explanation for awarding points is in **Item Fifty-One**. That item will give instructions for prioritizing recommendations in **Items Forty-Seven to Fifty**.

Each person is to individually do the work of prioritizing specific recommendations. Allow eight minutes. Next, have each person report scores to the recorder. After all have been reported, the group discusses its scores while the recorder tabulates the group score on each recommendation. This discussion and tabulation time is about seven minutes.

Have recorders share their tabulations with the large group. After all the reports, use a calculator to quickly report the total for each recommendation. Participants are to write in total scores on **Items Forty-Seven to Fifty**.

This information is to guide the leaders of the eldership in planning for ministry in the coming months. The records of tabulations are to be kept and displayed at leadership meetings.

Step 10 • 13 minutes   Purposes #1, #5
Evaluation

Offer a time for general comments. Prepare for the comments by using Item Fifty-Two.

After at least four minutes invite persons to relive highly positive moments in this course. Invite them to share as a total group the most valued learnings, new resolves, and affirmations of each other. Also, let the climate of sharing be open and free for expression of frustrations, unmet expectations, and advice on improving the course the next time it is offered.

Step 11 • 5 minutes   Purposes #1, #2, #4
Closing

Close by playing **Voice Impression 19** and having participants read along in **Item Fifty-Three**. Share the unison prayer in **Item Fifty-Four** and invite people to greet each other with hugs, handshakes, comments, and blessings in any style appropriate to that group and the mood of the moment.

NOTE: This section takes two hours with no break. It is advisable to allow two and one-half hours so that you will not feel cramped for time. After Step 8 may be a good fifteen-minute break period. Some groups will not complete this section in one session.

Eldership Meeting Agenda

1. A Community of Teaching and Learning

Sharing of personal news
Bible study and prayer
Report on educational activities and plans of the congregation

2. Shepherds

Report on calls and pastoral concerns of members
Training in specific types of pastoral visits
Prayers of intercession

3. Celebrants at the Lord's Table

Coordinating schedule on who serves which Sunday
Calendaring communion to shut-ins
Preview and dialogue on lectionary and worship themes for coming services
Review of training in serving communion and preparing prayers for the table

4. Overseers

Plan and/or report on support visits with leaders of functional committees and task groups
Share visions of what God is calling the congregation to be and do
Close with discussion on plans for next meeting and prayers for each other

This agenda is comprehensive. Not all steps will be covered in every meeting. For example, one meeting may be given just to Bible study, prayer, and a training exercise on making a hospital visit, and checking calendars for serving communion.

Another meeting may go briefly through Steps 1–3 and then spend a lot of time on Step 4. All sorts of options are available for those with flexibility. Needs will determine agenda.

The leader will need to pay close attention to the closing discussion on plans for the next meeting in order to do thorough preparation for the next gathering.

Elders' Retreat

Friday Evening	Section I, 7:00–9:30 p.m. Evening Prayer—Psalm 4
Saturday Morning	Morning Prayer—Psalm 116:1–11 Section II, 9:00–11:30 a.m.
Saturday Afternoon	Midday Prayer—Psalm 121 Section III, 1:00–4:00 p.m.
Saturday Evening	Section IV, 7:00–9:30 p.m. Evening Prayer—Psalm 91

Sunday Morning	Morning Prayer—Psalm 116:12–19
	Section V, 9:00–11:00 a.m.
	   (In session use scriptures planned for worship service)
	Worship
	   (In worship service used table prayers prepared in
	   Section V)

Sunday Afternoon	Section VI, 1:00–3:30 p.m. Use **Voice Impression 19** as part of closing worship

Leisure: A retreat is to have quiet times of rest as well as times of work. Give people choices of how to spend their leisure: playing games, reading, conversing, praying, napping.

Meals: What arrangements have been made for meals? It is advisable that retreat participants be free of meal preparation and cleanup. One idea is to have deacons plan, prepare, serve, and clean up the meals.

Prayers: An enriching part of any retreat is the time for silence and prayer. Encourage participants to use leisure time for prayer, walks, or for times of solitude and meditation.

Built into the units are prayers written by elders for use with the group. Also, the psalms are to be prayed at morning, midday, and evening prayer.

Someone may be able to teach the group simple chants for singing the psalms, or the group may be divided into two choirs for reading the psalms antiphonally by verses. Either chanting or reading, give people time to reflect silently on the psalm to be prayed and then to pray the psalm as a prayer of the community.

CPSIA information can be obtained at www.ICGtesting.com
Printed in the USA
LVOW092046080313

323348LV00002B/8/P